Sin, Pride & Self-Acceptance

THE PROBLEM OF IDENTITY IN THEOLOGY & PSYCHOLOGY

Terry D. Cooper

IVP Academic

An imprint of InterVarsity Press
Downers Grove, Illinois

InterVarsity Press
P.O. Box 1400, Downers Grove, IL 60515-1426
World Wide Web: www.ivpress.com
E-mail: email@ivpress.com

InterVarsity Press® is the book-publishing division of InterVarsity Christian Fellowship/USA®, a movement of students and faculty active on campus at hundreds of universities, colleges and schools of nursing in the United States of America, and a member movement of the International Fellowship of Evangelical Students. For information about local and regional activities, write Public Relations Dept., InterVarsity Christian Fellowship/USA, 6400 Schroeder Rd., P.O. Box 7895, Madison, WI 53707-7895, or visit the IVCF website at <www.intervarsity.org>.

Scripture quotations, unless otherwise noted, are from the New Revised Standard Version of the Bible, copyright 1989 by the Division of Christian Education of the National Council of the Churches of Christ in the USA. Used by permission. All rights reserved.

Cover design: Kathleen Lay Burrows

Cover image: Lise Metzger/Getty Images

ISBN 978-0-8308-2728-2

Printed in the United States of America ∞

Library of Congress Cataloging-in-Publication Data

Cooper, Terry D.
  Sin, pride, and self-acceptance: the problem of identity in
  theology
and psychology/Terry D. Cooper.
    p. cm.
Includes bibliographical references and indexes.
  ISBN 0-8308-2728-5 (pbk.: alk. paper)
  1. Pride and vanity. 2. Self-esteem—Religious
aspects—Christianity.
3. Niebuhr, Reinhold, 1892-1971. 4. Rogers, Carl R. (Carl Ransom),
1902- 5. Sin—Psychology. I. Title.
  BV4627.P7C66 2003
  233'.5—dc221

                                               2003006749

| P | 20 | 19 | 18 | 17 | 16 | 15 | 14 | 13 | 12 | 11 | 10 | 9 | 8 | 7 | 6 | 5 |
| Y | 26 | 25 | 24 | 23 | 22 | 21 | 20 | 19 | 18 | 17 | 16 | 15 | 14 | 13 |

For my wife,

Linda Maria Cooper,

with love and a grateful heart

CONTENTS

ACKNOWLEDGMENTS

I wish to thank several people for offering valuable input into this book. From Marty Maddox, James Fisher and Beldon Lane I learned much about Reinhold Niebuhr. From Rob Anderson and Paul Dukro I had great assistance in understanding Carl Rogers and humanistic psychology. In Robert Asa I found an excellent dialogue partner concerning the work of Karen Horney. And from Patout Burns and Matt Becker I have been much informed about Augustine and the Augustinian tradition. My deep thanks goes to each of these persons.

I finished much of this book when I was on sabbatical at Emory University in the spring of 2002. I want to thank St. Louis Community College-Meramec and particularly my dean, Walter Clark, and my department chair, Fredna Scroggins, for their support in making this sabbatical possible. I also wish to thank Emory University for the warm reception I received during my sabbatical. I particularly want to thank Rod Hunter, Karen Scheib, Luke Timothy Johnson, Steve Tipton, Brian Mahan, James Fowler and John Patton for stimulating conversations.

I am also appreciative of the support I have received from Dennis Klass at Webster University. Denny has greatly encouraged me to create undergraduate classes at the intersection of psychology and religious studies, and some of the ideas in this book reflect those stimulating classes.

In addition, I am grateful for the excellent work of my editor, Gary Deddo. Gary is not only a fine scholar but a warm and extremely efficient editor. The entire group at IVP has been most encouraging and helpful in this writing effort.

I want to especially thank Don Browning, with whom I have worked closely over the past year. When it comes to the relationship of psychology and Christian thought, I know of no one with a more comprehensive understanding. The key insights I have learned from Don have been matched by the warm and gracious generosity of both Don and his lovely wife, Carol.

I am very appreciative of the ongoing support I receive from my parents, Don and Barbara Cooper, as well as two gifted stepdaughters, Lori and Michelle Lampert. I am also indebted to the many conversations I have had concerning the relationship between psychology and religion with Dan Reynolds, David Johnson, "Bud" Peyton, Michael and Hazel Jackson, Rick Wilson, Danny Denning, Steve May, Richard Hutch, Dale Bengtson, Britt-Mari Sykes, Barbara Bennett, Mike Rusnac, Jim Bradley and the late James Armour. For each of these friends and conversational partners I am indeed grateful.

And perhaps most significant of all, I wish to thank my wife, partner and friend, Linda Maria Cooper, to whom I have dedicated this book. A wonderful teacher, Linda's passion for the education of children is a regular inspiration in my life. She has encouraged and supported this book all the way. Thanks, Linda.

INTRODUCTION

Recently, I have heard conversations similar to this one between two people I'll call Sam and Betty.

"I find it very hard to tolerate Jack," said Sam. "He's extremely pompous, full of himself and conceited. Who does he think he is? He really thinks he's better than everyone else."

"Yes," said Betty, "but you know that's all a big mask to cover his real problem—low self-esteem. It may look like he's arrogant, but the real issue is deeper than that. Down deep, I'll bet he really doesn't accept himself."

"Are you kidding?" responded Sam. "That guy has too much self-esteem. I don't think he's insecure at all. In fact, he has something of a God-complex."

"But can't you see underneath all that, Sam?" asked Betty. "Jack is like everyone else—his basic problem is low self-esteem, which he hides very well."

Sam quickly retorted, "I can't believe you think everyone's problem is low self-esteem! Particularly in today's world! I think the exact opposite is true. People today think too highly of themselves. They place themselves at the center of everything. In fact, they love themselves so much that they have nothing left over to give anybody else."

"But what makes you assume that?"

"Look around you, Betty. Self-centeredness is everywhere. And even though it seems worse today, it's an age-old problem. Pride is our number one enemy, the first and greatest sin. Both Judaism and Christianity have always taught this."

"Yes," said Betty, "but that was before psychotherapists really started understanding that pride is a cover-up for feelings of inadequacy. My friend, who is a psychologist, says that all her patients, down deep, have low self-esteem."

"But that's easy to say when you're working in counseling," argued Sam. "Counselors look for low self-esteem and always find it. Then they think that it is everybody's problem. Of course people who go to counseling are temporarily down on themselves. But as soon as their lives get back on track, pride will probably take over again."

"But I think pride is never the bottom-line issue," said Betty. "It's not the *primary* problem. Instead, it's a symptom."

"I see it as the *primary* problem," argued Sam, "and I think this is where religion and psychology often differ. Psychology minimizes the problem of sin or excessive self-regard."

"I disagree. I think sin is more likely to come from a failure to accept myself than exaggerated pride in myself."

"I'm sorry, but I find that view really naive."

"And Sam," said Betty, "I find your view cynical."

Beneath this discussion between Sam and Betty are two very different perspectives on humanity's most basic problem. Sam's view focuses on pride as the driving force in human behavior. Human beings have a distorted inclination to think of themselves more highly than they should. This perspective is part of a rich theological tradition in Christianity that was especially emphasized by the fifth-century theologian Augustine. Taking his lead from the apostle Paul, especially in Romans, Augustine argued that human pride is an attempt to replace God as the center of our existence. As we replace a trust in God with a complete reliance on self, we commit idolatry. We were never meant to be the center of our own existence, and once we deify ourselves, our lives become very disordered. This Augustinian perspective finds powerful expression in the writings of twentieth-century theologian and social ethicist Reinhold Niebuhr.

Betty, on the other hand, believes that pride is never the most basic problem. A prideful demeanor is an attempt to compensate for deeper feelings of inadequacy. Thinking "too highly of ourselves" appears as a symptom. Beneath the pride lies feelings of inadequacy and often self-contempt. Betty believes she has the support of contemporary psychotherapy in seeing people in this way. Sin is not inordinate self-regard but instead a failure to be a self, an underdeveloped self or a lack of self-acceptance. Betty believes that the destructive things people do to each other can ultimately be traced back to a refusal to accept themselves as they are. Calling pride the primary problem is superficial and lacks a deeper understanding of the dynamics of sin.

Our assumptions about whether pride or low self-esteem is the primary human problem deeply influence our approach to people. If we assume that pride is primary, our approach may be more confrontational, more direct, more concerned to help others acknowledge and accept their inadequacies, limitations and sins. Ministers who support this view for instance, will be less "delicate" in their sermons. They will not fear offending the already wounded egos of their parishioners. Counselors who believe in the primacy of pride will often be more inclined to point out a client's distorted perceptions of themselves rather than support, nurture and build up a beleaguered self-concept. Exaggerated self-claims, feelings of entitlement and a disregard for others will be focal points of therapy.

On the other hand, ministers convinced that deep-rooted feelings of inadequacy represent the primary problem will talk less about sin and much more about the importance of embracing ourselves as we are. Their ministry will be based on support, nurture and encouragement, rather than confrontation about our self-centeredness. In turn, counselors convinced that we undervalue ourselves will focus on empathy, warmth and affirmation of our strengths. Both clergy and counselors will assume that we are already hard enough on ourselves, so they need not add to our self-condemnation. Why kick someone who is already down?

Beliefs about the pride versus low self-esteem issue will also greatly influence how parents go about the process of raising their children. If they assume that we human beings have a tendency toward proud self-assertion and disregard for others, parents will be concerned with developing limits and structure to their children's abounding energy. They will more readily recognize the importance of discipline. Since they do not see the major childhood problem as low self-esteem, they will be less afraid to directly confront their kids about misbehavior. They will not worry about wounding a child's creative spirit by saying "no."

Parents who believe in the low self-esteem inclinations of their children will work hard to build up their children's sense of worth. The most important focus of their parenting will be helping their children "feel good about themselves." They will often attempt to avoid saying anything that might create negative self-perceptions in their children.

Parents who believe in the primacy of pride may look at parents who hold the low self-esteem perspective and say the following: "You are enabling a generation of children who have self-esteem alright, but at everyone else's expense. These kids have little concern for anyone else, don't know the meaning of the word *no* and feel entitled to uninterrupted self-indulgence. Preoccupied with helping them 'feel good about themselves,' you've created kids who are selfish and greedy and who lack boundaries. Things like sacrifice and concern for others won't be a part of their lives."

Parents who believe the primary problem is low self-esteem may respond as follows: "Most kids act out, do destructive things and become self-centered because they have never felt accepted or accepted themselves. Rigid expectations and demands of children create strong feelings of inadequacy. When children don't like themselves, they are often damaging to others. Kids respond to support, encouragement and the freedom to be themselves. As they learn to love and respect themselves, they will then be able to love and respect others."

This same difference can be seen in the world of education. If college professors assume that first-year college students struggle with low self-esteem, they may strongly encourage them to express their perspectives and gain greater awareness of their thoughts about certain issues. Their focus will be on helping these students trust their own reasoning capacities and have greater confidence in their academic skills. Rather than sheepishly avoiding an opinion, students will be encouraged to be more self-assertive. If they don't do well on exams, professors will need to work hard to build their self-esteem because these students will likely consider themselves a failure.

If we assume the overvalued self perspective, however, we may notice that many college students enter classes with an overabundance of naive trust in their own opinions. These students tend to be ethnocentric and self-righteous about the certainty of their belief systems. We may see our task as challenging the inflated nature of their claims, helping them see the limitations of their thought processes and insisting that they hear other perspectives as well. If they do not do well on our exams, they will likely say the exam is unfair or that our teaching is defective. The last thing they will do is blame themselves.

Whether in preaching, counseling, parenting or educating, this assumption about the core problem of the human condition raises its head. Our beliefs concerning this issue to a great extent structure our ways of approaching others.

THE DIRECTION OF THIS BOOK

My task in this book will be as follows. First, I will examine more carefully how this debate over pride versus self-contempt has divided many thinkers in both psychology and theology. In the first chapter, I attempt to get to the core of these differences. Along the way, I will point out that this issue, while seemingly new, is a very old debate within the Christian community and the culture at large.

Chapter two puts forth the Augustinian pride argument as developed in the twentieth-century theologian and social ethicist Reinhold Niebuhr. The rich analysis in Niebuhr's theological anthropology, his appropriation and critique of Freud and his vision of the intricacies of pride will be laid out.

I will then turn, in chapter three, to how this Augustinian pride perspective understands the problem of self-indulgence, compulsivity and addiction. How does the pride thesis handle the issue of sensuality? The relationship between Augustine's classic understanding of concupiscence and Gerald May's notion of universal addiction will be explored.

Next, in chapter four, I will examine feminist critiques of the Augustinian model. A group of important feminist theologians have argued that the Augustinian-Niebuhrian model may be appropriate for most men, but it does not adequately describe women's experience. Excessive self-regard is not their problem.

Chapter five will look at humanistic psychology's assumption, found most clearly in Carl Rogers, that pride is never the primary problem for *anyone,* male or female. I will examine how Rogers describes the self-contempt typical of the clients with whom he worked. I will then raise the question of whether or not a Christian understanding of sin can be built around the Rogerian framework.

In chapter six, after having pointed out the polar opposition in the pride and self-contempt issue, I will employ the work of Karen Horney, who argues that pride and self-contempt are always two sides of the same process.

In other words, it is never an either-or phenomenon. Horney's work points toward the intermingling of the experiences of pride and self-contempt.

And finally, in the last chapter, I will attempt to pull the insights together into an integrative whole. Here, for instance, I will argue that while the Augustinian tradition needs the input of the feminist perspective, it is also true that many feminists have perhaps missed Niebuhr's subtle and undeveloped notion of sensuality, which includes self-abnegation and self-avoidance. I will further argue that any comprehensive view of the human condition needs to see pride and self-contempt as dual processes, very closely related.

The goal of this effort is to move us toward a more comprehensive self-understanding and a more fully developed grasp of the dynamics of human sin. For it is in the context of this understanding of sin that grace becomes even more meaningful. Clearly this is a project at the intersection of psychology and Christian theology, where I believe there are rich opportunities for dialogue. My hope is to aid in that discussion.

PRIDE AND
SELF-CONTEMPT

Many of us interested in both Christian theology and psychology often come to a crossroads on our journey. Frequently our theological understanding of the dynamics of sin is greatly influenced by the Augustinian tradition with its accent on pride as the primary human problem. This tradition asserts that as we refuse to trust God, we substitute ourselves as the center of our existence. Ignoring our Creator, we egocentrically attempt to control reality. We think more highly of ourselves than is warranted. From this angle, grandiosity is the self's nagging tendency. Conceit and arrogance are natural outgrowths of not realizing our limitations in relationship to our Source as well as others. Humility and care for others are the important qualities lacking in our self-preoccupations and self-elevations. Within the Judeo-Christian tradition, this self-centeredness is a form of idolatry identified as sin. This inevitably throws our lives out of balance. Various inordinate desires or addictions emerge because we have lost our center in God. Pride, or God-replacement, is our primary problem.

Yet many of us have also experienced problems with low self-esteem or deep-rooted feelings of inadequacy. These problems don't quite match the Augustinian pride portrait. Out of negative feelings about ourselves, we may have consulted the helping professions, which are often highly influenced by the humanistic psychotherapies. We've been told that far from having a problem with pride, we are struggling with self-hatred and a need for self-acceptance. Surely the Augustinian emphasis on pride is wrong. Our major problem is low self-esteem or even self-contempt. Destructive, hurtful behavior toward others stems from this negative view of ourselves. We cannot love others, we are told, until we love ourselves. This low evaluation of self must be transformed into self-acceptance. Then, and only then, will we be able to respond to others in a healthy manner. Thinking of ourselves more highly than we should is not our basic problem; instead, our predicament involves a low evaluation of ourselves. Again, the Augustinian pride thesis is wrong.

Throughout much of the twentieth century, these two views of the self and its most fundamental problem have been in conflict. Psychoanalyst Erich Fromm, for instance, departs from Freud by insisting that low self-esteem, a lack of self-love or even self-contempt is our primary problem.[1] For Fromm, self-love does not always lead to narcissism. According to Freud, however, self-love is the turning of the libido back on ourselves. Hence, self-love and love of others are antagonistic. Put differently, if we love ourselves, we have nothing left for others.

Moving away from this position, Fromm argues that a profound distinction exists between "self-love" and "selfishness." He states it eloquently:

> Selfishness and self-love, far from being identical, are actually opposites. The selfish person does not love himself too much but too little; in fact he hates himself. This lack of fondness and care for himself, which is only one expression of his lack of productiveness, leaves him empty and frustrated. He is necessarily unhappy and anxiously concerned to snatch from life the satisfactions which he blocks himself from attaining. He seems to care too much for himself, but actually he only makes an unsuccessful attempt to cover up and compensate for his failure to care for his real self. Freud holds that the selfish person is narcissistic, as if he had withdrawn his love from others and turned it toward his own person. It is true that selfish persons are incapable of loving others, but they are not capable of loving themselves either.[2]

---

[1] Erich Fromm, *The Art of Loving* (New York: Harper & Row, 1956).
[2] Ibid., p. 51.

Thus, unlike Freud, Fromm believes that self-love is pivotal for our ability to love others. Again, self-love is not the enemy of caring for others. Instead, it is a *lack* of self-love that sets the stage for a devouring self-preoccupation. This, in turn, leads to an exalted view of our own importance. Thus, pride is not the most basic problem as the Augustinian tradition has stressed.

Fromm finds agreement among other psychotherapists. Theodore Rubin, for instance, describes the manner in which self-contempt, rather than self-love, is humanity's primary enemy:

> People will actively depreciate, demean, and put themselves down generally, with almost complete ease and with little or no awareness of the destructive aspects and results involved. The same people may speak of feeling demoralized, depleted, weak, helpless, hopeless, frightened, vulnerable, fragile, incapable, or self-doubting, without making any connection at all between these symptoms and their own attacks upon themselves.[3]

Rubin further adds that "all neurotic manifestations are in fact incarnations of self-hate."[4] He speaks for a wide section of the helping professions.

Psychoanalyst Ralph Greenson, on the other hand, maintains the Freudian position that self-love is dangerous.[5] He argues that self-love involves a "turning in on oneself" in such a manner that outward investments of love become impossible. While he recognizes the importance of self-respect and self-care, he adamantly resists notions of "self-love."

Neo-Freudian Alfred Adler believes that feelings of inferiority are inevitable and built into the very structure of human development.[6] The mere fact that we each begin our lives as small creatures while adults tower over us provokes feelings of inferiority. Also, it may seem to children that adults are in complete control of their fate. In other words, our feelings of inadequacy as we try to move about in an adult world have biological roots. This

---

[3]Theodore Rubin, *Compassion and Self-Hate* (New York: David McKay, 1975), p. 29.
[4]Ibid., p. 133.
[5]Ralph Greenson, *The Technique and Practice of Psychoanalysis* (New York: International Universities Press, 1968).
[6]Alfred Adler, *The Science of Living* (New York: Doubleday, 1969).

sense of inadequacy, however, is not pathological if it can be a prodding source of motivation for excellence. It can trigger a striving for self-mastery.

The problem is that for some individuals this feeling of natural inferiority does not promote a striving for superiority. Instead, it leaves them feeling weak, powerless, inadequate and even hopeless. To compensate for these pathological feelings, a "superiority complex" is erected.[7] Because the feelings of inferiority fail to motivate a movement toward growth and are instead a devastating indictment, some individuals develop a false sense of superiority. This is a spurious mask used to escape the fears of inadequacy, a compensation for a sense of failure.

For Adler, once again, some feelings of inferiority are healthy. However, when those feelings cluster into an inferiority *complex,* development is arrested and enormous energy is poured into maintaining the "superior" image. It is not "normal" to have a superiority complex. It is normal to strive for superiority in the sense that we each ambitiously strive to be our best. Yet an inflated image of ourselves always has deep-rooted feelings of inferiority working behind the scenes. So, an overvalued self, for Adler, is an attempt to escape the painful negative feelings concerning our true worth.

The emergence of humanistic psychology in the twentieth century strongly emphasized the problems of an undervalued self. A basic sense of inadequacy, often internalized early in life, sets the stage for negative feelings toward ourselves. Unfortunately, even well-intentioned families often communicate conditional acceptance to children. These "conditions of worth" invariably lead them to believe in their own inadequacy. Humanistic approaches to psychotherapy are based on the assumption that the self desperately needs nurture, support and acceptance in order to gain self-regard. Carl Rogers, Abraham Maslow and Fritz Perls have been significant leaders in a movement that quickly became part of popular culture. It flooded bookstores with titles on how to love ourselves, take care of ourselves, nurture ourselves and gain self-esteem. The underlying message seemed to be that *everyone* has a problem with a deep-rooted sense of inferiority.

This notion of low self-esteem as the fundamental human dilemma also spread into churches and synagogues throughout America. Sermons be-

---

[7]Ibid., p. 31.

came less focused on confronting parishioners about their egocentricity and far more focused on addressing the "real" issue—a failure to love themselves. Perhaps Robert Schuller became the most visible of a new breed of clergy looking more at our feelings of inadequacy than our pride. The conviction seemed to be the same, whether in ecclesiastical communities or the helping professions: people need to learn to value themselves. Once we do that, most of the other problems we face will take care of themselves.

Educational institutions and parents also became very concerned with children's self-esteem. This was the key for unlocking each child's potential, a way of tapping the natural resources within each person. Teachers and parents tried to ensure that kids "felt good about themselves."

In addition, a new clinical interest emerged concerning the problem of shame.[8] Much of the literature identifies shame as something quite different from guilt, with which it has often been lumped together. Toxic shame, as it is often called, is the condition of feeling flawed, defective and inadequate as a person. It is a deeper problem than guilt in that it attacks *us* rather than our behavior. Guilt has the more limited task of pointing out what we have *done*. Not content with that, shame indicts us for who we *are*. Developmentally, it precedes guilt because shame can be experienced even before a child understands the differences between right and wrong. Put simply, it is saying "*I* am bad," even before I am able to understand that what I *did* was bad. It convicts the entire self. Its purpose is exposure and condemnation, not education.

Through PBS specials and popular psychological literature, individuals such as John Bradshaw focused public attention on this problem of shame. This is, of course, another way of talking about low self-esteem or a negative view of self. Bradshaw's bestseller *Healing the Shame That Binds You* diagnoses shame as the universal human dilemma. Childhood experience *before* the shaming process began is understood as a state of pure innocence, not unlike the Garden of Eden before the Fall.[9] Unfortunately, shame is in-

---

[8]Much of this work has been popularized by individuals such as John Bradshaw. See especially his *Healing the Shame That Binds You* (Deerfield Beach, Fla.: Health Communications, 1988). Much of Bradshaw's work is based on Gershen Kaufman's *Shame: The Power of Caring* (Rochester, Vt.: Schenkman, 1980).

[9]Terry D. Cooper, "The Psychotherapeutic Evangelism of John Bradshaw," *Pastoral Psychology* 44, no. 2 (1995): 73-82.

ternalized and, consequently, needs to be healed. Thus, this "original pain," as Bradshaw calls it, replaces the traditional theological understanding of "original sin."[10] The point is that this process is something that is done *to* us. It is an outside-in maneuver. "Salvation," for Bradshaw, is closely tied to grieving what was done to us and reconnecting with this original state of innocence he calls "the inner child."[11]

This understanding of a fall into toxic shame differs from a traditional strand in Christian thought that emphasizes *our* responsibility for our dilemma. Typically, in the Christian tradition, our fall is tied up with our own freedom and often with the refusal to trust God in the face of anxiety. It is not so much a story about what is done *to us* as it is a story of our own mishandled anxiety. To put it directly, this traditional viewpoint would say the following to our culture: "Look, it does not matter if we have perfect, non-shaming parents, schools that offer nothing but encouragement and overall environments that are quite therapeutic. We still have the problem within ourselves—namely, acting in destructive ways because of the anxiety that is simply part of being human." At times, Bradshaw seems to move toward Pelagianism in his belief that if we could simply correct faulty parenting and eliminate the shaming process, children would live "above" dysfunction.[12] This seems to minimize the internal conflict that inevitably arises no matter what the external conditions. A central theme in the Adamic story is that the first couple *had* a healthy situation, yet they still acted in self-centered ways. While Bradshaw provides a much-needed awareness of the importance of a nurturing environment, he seems, at times, to minimize the power of the self's capacity to act destructively even in ideal circumstances. This optimistic tendency in the humanistic perspective, which Bradshaw has certainly absorbed, will be critiqued in more detail later.

The differences between the overvalued and undervalued self are not simply a tension between religion's pessimism and psychotherapy's optimism, however. This split exists within each of the disciplines. Freud, espe-

---

[10]Ibid., p. 75

[11]Ibid., p. 80.

[12]This reference to Pelagianism points toward the fifth-century monk Pelagius, who believed that human beings are capable of keeping God's commandments without any additional assistance from God's grace.

cially in his later writings, certainly emphasized a rather dismal portrait of the self.[13] The primitive impulses of the id must be checked by social restraint or civilization would not be possible.[14] Inordinate self-love, selfishness and aggression are natural inclinations within the human psyche. These must be restrained and controlled. The id has no self-regulating capacity, so without the benefit of social restraint, we would all be savages. Such is the nature of our primitive instinctuality.

Against this Freudian pessimism about human nature, the humanistic psychologies of Rogers, Maslow, Perls and others were framed. There were, of course, others such as Jung, Horney and Fromm who had a less negative view of personhood and who helped make the emergence of humanistic psychology possible. But it is hard to overestimate the radical differences between a Freudian and Rogerian perspective of the self. Rogers's biographer, Howard Kirschenbaum, sums up this difference in a quote by Rogers:

> So when a Freudian such as Karl Menninger tells me (as he has, in a discussion of this issue) that he perceives man as "innately destructive," I can only shake my head in wonderment. It leads me to all kinds of perplexing questions. How could it be that Menninger and I, working with such intimate relationships with individuals in distress, experience people so differently?[15]

Rogers goes on to make an interesting speculation about why he and Freud differ so much in their basic views of the self. Admitting that this is only a hypothesis, Rogers suggests that even though Freud came to understand some of his own hidden dimensions through self-analysis, he was not able to fully accept those dimensions on his own. In fact, all of us are limited in what we can discover on our own. Once patterns of self-depreciation have been established, it takes another person to empathize with our inward journey in order for full self-acceptance to be possible. As brilliant as Freud's self-analysis was, it lacked the warmly accepting relationship that makes the disowned parts of the self easier to embrace. Rogers continues his speculation:

---

[13]Sigmund Freud, *Civilizations and Its Discontents,* trans. James Strachey (New York: W. W. Norton, 1963).
[14]Ibid.
[15]Howard Kirschenbaum, *On Becoming Carl Rogers* (New York: Delta Books, 1979), p. 250.

Hence, though he might come to know and to some extent understand the hidden and denied aspects of himself, I question whether
he could ever come to accept them fully, to embrace them as a meaningful, acceptable, and constructive part of himself. More likely he
continued to perceive them unacceptable aspects of himself—enemies, whom knowing he could control—rather than as impulses
which, when existing freely in balance with his other impulses, were
constructive. At any rate I regard this as a hypothesis worthy of con-
sideration.[16]

While Freudians might wince at such a statement, it grows out of Rogers's deep conviction that we discover ourselves most deeply in relationship
to an accepting other. Hence, Freud's attempt to achieve self-acceptance in
the isolation of his own analysis is similar to Luther's attempt to gain a sense
of grace through the ascetic practices in a monastery. To put it religiously,
we cannot muster up our own grace. It has to be mediated to us by a power
of acceptance greater than we are.

PSYCHOLOGICAL CRITICS OF
THE "LOW SELF-ESTEEM" ARGUMENT

Psychological perspectives other than Freudian ones are also critical of humanistic psychotherapy's optimistic evaluation of the self. An example is the
work of Paul Vitz, whose not-so-subtly titled book *Psychology as Religion:
The Cult of Self-Worship* came out in 1977 and was revised in 1994.[17] As the
title indicates, Vitz believes that selfist psychology has become a secularized
religion of self-adoration. By "selfist psychology" he refers primarily to the
influence of Rogers, Maslow, Rollo May and Fromm.[18] He argues that a
radical preoccupation with individual rights has led our culture to believe
that concepts such as duty, obligation, restraint or inhibition are rooted in a
primitive way of thinking. Vitz attacks the core of the human potential
movement—namely, the belief in the innate goodness of the self or the actualizing tendency. He argues that the forces emerging from biological evo-

---

[16]Ibid., p. 251.
[17]Paul Vitz, *Psychology as Religion: The Cult of Self-Worship*, 2nd ed. (Grand Rapids, Mich.: Eerdmans,
    1994).
[18]Ibid.

lution do not reveal the kind of one-directional growth tendency that is a sacred assumption in humanistic psychology.

For Vitz, self-esteem is not our primary problem. In fact, a genetic tendency toward selfishness may well blind us to the collective moral wisdom of the past.[19] Vitz believes that humanistic psychologists such as Rogers blame the social order for trying to sabotage human growth and expansion. Society is accused of distorting the individual's basic goodness. But the human potential movement forgets that the social order is humanly constructed and maintained.[20]

As an experimental psychologist, Vitz is upset that the humanistic psychotherapies are trying to ride on the coattails of psychological science. However, he does not think this unscientific optimism is limited to psychology. It has appeared in various religious circles as well. In fact, he believes that antecedents to humanistic psychology lie in the Protestant liberalism of the earlier part of the twentieth century. Vitz thinks one of the precursors of humanistic psychology was New York minister Harry Emerson Fosdick. His widely read book *On Becoming a Real Person,* written twenty years before Carl Rogers's *On Becoming a Person,* offers familiar themes for Rogers's later book.[21] Both Fosdick and Norman Vincent Peale made self-fulfillment a central thrust of their theologies.[22] In fact, according to Vitz, Fosdick admits that the idea of *integration* seems to have replaced the concept of *salvation.*[23] The important thing to remember here is that the notion of self-realization was heavily preached from New York pulpits. For Fosdick, all of us have a basic urge toward wholeness. Sin is more a matter of confusion and lack of focus than an inclination toward evil.[24] Integration, for Fosdick, derives from self-discovery, self-acceptance and self-love.

---

[19]Vitz has been heavily influenced here by Donald Campbell's 1974 Presidential Address to the American Psychological Association, later published as "On the Conflicts Between Biological and Social Evolution and Between Psychology and Moral Tradition," *American Psychologist* 30 (December 1974): 1103-26.

[20]Terry D. Cooper, "Self-Awareness or Self-Absorption: How the Sociology of Knowledge Can Help Counselors," *Counseling and Values* 26, no. 4 (1982): 275-80.

[21]Harry Emerson Fosdick, *On Becoming a Real Person* (New York: Harper & Row, 1943); Carl R. Rogers, *On Becoming a Person* (Boston: Houghton Mifflin, 1961).

[22]See, for example, Harry Emerson Fosdick, *As I See Religion* (New York: Harper & Row, 1932); Norman Vincent Peale, *The Art of Living* (New York: Abingdon-Cokesbury, 1937).

[23]Harry Fosdick, cited in Vitz, *Psychology as Religion,* pp. 99-103.

[24]Vitz, *Psychology as Religion,* pp. 99-103.

I believe that Vitz overstates the case that Rogerian therapy automatically leads to self-worship. In fact, self-worship contradicts the very nature of what both Maslow and Rogers identify as self-actualization. Self-actualizing individuals are focused on a project or vision larger than the self. They never make self-actualization their primary goal. Vitz overlooks the significant number of people who have been liberated *from* self-preoccupation through Rogerian therapy. These are individuals who have found in an empathic relationship the ability to accept those parts of themselves that they had disowned and that had kept them self-obsessed. In short, Vitz completely ignores the implicit discovery of grace in Rogerian therapy. As Thomas Oden and Don Browning have pointed out so well, the Rogerian therapist often mediates a level of acceptance that is ultimately grounded in God.[25] Part of what has traditionally been called a "bondage to sin" is indeed a prison of self-preoccupation in which we are struggling to be acceptable. The release from this captivity can be a powerful experience in the presence of one who implicitly mediates our ontological acceptance. Instead of encouraging self-worship, this can free us to live, care for others and get on with our lives without excessive self-focus.

Nevertheless, Vitz has written an interesting and challenging book that calls into question the possible naivete of the whole self-help culture. Surely he is accurate in pointing toward a tendency in our culture to make our own private "growth" the most important thing in the world. Whether or not it is fair, however, to lay that at the doorstep of Rogers or Maslow is quite another matter, one we will investigate later.

David Myers is another respected psychological voice who opposes the thesis that an undervalued self is humanity's primary problem. In his major works on the topic, *The Inflated Self, Psychology Through the Eyes of Faith* and his frequently used text, *Social Psychology,* he argues precisely the opposite point.[26] Instead of depending on the Freudian pessimism concerning the human condition, Myers believes that research in social psychology confirms a traditional biblical portrait of humanity as fundamentally selfish and

---

[25]Thomas C. Oden, *Kerygma and Counseling* (Philadelphia: Westminster Press, 1966); Don S. Browning, *Atonement and Psychotherapy* (Philadelphia: Westminster Press, 1966).

[26]David G. Myers, *The Inflated Self* (New York: Seabury Press, 1980); *Psychology Through the Eyes of Faith* (San Francisco: Harper & Row, 1987); *Social Psychology,* 5th ed. (New York: McGraw-Hill, 1996).

self-centered.[27] As one of his titles obviously implies, Myers sees the basic human problem as self-inflation rather than self-degradation. In other words, we think too highly of ourselves. Like Vitz, Myers believes that humanistic psychology has compounded our problems by its thesis that low self-esteem is our most basic problem. Unwarranted pride and egotism are the real dangers.

Myers proclaims that the findings of research psychology are quite sobering. They tend to challenge rather than build up the human ego. As Myers puts it, "To us proud individuals in a self-righteous culture, it is shocking to discover that one of the brute facts of human nature is our capacity for illusion and self-deception."[28] We are easily corrupted by a self-serving bias. This blinds us to an accurate picture of ourselves as well as the world. For Myers, this tendency toward selfishness is aptly demonstrated by evolutionary psychologists such as David Barash and Donald Campbell.[29] Myers believes the findings of evolutionary psychology support his thesis that pride and selfishness are primary, though he balks at the position that they are "built into" our basic nature. As a Christian psychologist, he believes the human condition is somehow a fallen one, and he contends that if selfishness is part of our original makeup, then we cannot really be held morally responsible for it.

Social psychologists have been the ones to provide convincing evidence that this selfish tendency exists. They have found this self-serving bias in both individual and group attitudes. This self-serving bias can especially be seen in attribution theory, which deals with how each person or group explains or accounts for their own and others' behavior. Put directly, to what do we *attribute* our behavior? Sometimes it is ourselves and sometimes it is others. Myers believes that these studies conclusively reveal a pattern. We humans tend to attribute positive behaviors to ourselves and negative behaviors to external factors. We take credit for the good things that happen to us and blame the bad things on outside considerations. A self-serving, self-justifying tendency is apparent. "Although it is popularly believed that most people suffer from the 'I'm not OK-You're OK' syndrome, research

---

[27]Myers, *Inflated Self.*
[28]Ibid., p. xiv.
[29]Ibid., p. 25.

indicates that William Saroyan was much closer to the truth: 'Every man is a good man in a bad world—as he himself knows.'"[30]

So we tend to accept credit for our successes and blame outside factors for our failures. Almost invariably, for instance, students who do well on an exam attribute it to their hard study and intelligence. When they do poorly, however, they often argue that the test was not a reliable indicator of their knowledge or ability. Other studies have indicated a tendency to overvalue the accuracy of our beliefs and judgments.[31] Myers is convinced these studies demonstrate that individuals are far more troubled by a superiority complex than an inferiority one. We regularly see ourselves, at least according to conscious report, in a far better light than we see others. In one survey of college faculty, for instance, 94 percent saw themselves as better than the average colleague.[32] In survey after survey, self-report indicated a very high estimate of self in comparison to others. Myers makes this interesting remark:

> Note how radically at odds this conclusion is with the popular wisdom that most of us suffer from low self-esteem and high self-disparagement. We are, to be sure, strongly motivated to maintain and enhance our self-esteem and we will welcome any message which helps us do that. But most of us are not groveling about with feelings that everyone else is better than we are. Preachers who deliver ego-boosting pep talks to audiences who are supposedly plagued with miserable self-images are preaching to a problem that seldom exists.[33]

Myers *does* recognize, however, that some individuals genuinely suffer from low self-esteem. He further believes that these are the persons likely to show up in a therapist's office. What he objects to, however, is the therapist generalizing from these interactions that low self-esteem must be *the* human problem. Again, persons with low self-esteem are a very small segment of our culture.

It is precisely at this point that social psychologists and psychotherapists often bump heads. In hearing about the evidence for a "superiority com-

---

[30]William Saroyan, quoted in Myers, *Inflated Self,* p. 21.
[31]See Myers, *Psychology Through the Eyes of Faith,* especially chap. 21.
[32]Ibid.
[33]Myers, *Inflated Self,* p. 24.

plex" in social psychology research, many psychotherapists are likely to respond, "Of course individuals will sound this way in the context of a survey where their defenses are up." They will often tell a researcher what they would *like* to believe about themselves or what may sound like self-confident healthiness. But it is in the safe environment of psychotherapy, not a cold, quick interview process, that we discover what people really think about themselves. Thus, psychotherapists have an opportunity to get to know individuals at their deepest levels because they are privy to a world unknown to social research. When the defenses begin to drop and the person reveals what is going on below the surface, many therapists find that the primary problem is *not* self-inflation.

Social psychologists will no doubt reply that psychotherapy disclosure represents a temporary condition of persons who have been wounded by life and appear broken. Put simply, they are "down on themselves." But are these persons this way outside of the one or two hours each week that they are in therapy? Further, even if these individuals legitimately struggle with low self-esteem, countless others in our society would not go near a psychotherapist's office because they do not believe they have "problems." These persons attribute their difficulties to the environment or to others.

Psychotherapists will then counter that this so-called sense of superiority is a thin veneer born out of defensiveness and self-alienation. These persons have learned to hide their woundedness and deep-seated feelings of inadequacy behind a facade of social confidence. Peel it off, and we will find an anxious individual who is trying to cope behind a mask of security. In short, only when the aching issue of the unacceptable self has been addressed are we free to get on with our lives without a gnawing self-preoccupation. Pain in my leg absorbs me until I deal with it. Once it has been medically addressed, I can then walk away from the hospital without thinking about it.

Yet for Myers, "The self-serving bias is the social psychologist's new rendition of the forever underappreciated truth about human pride."[34] He sees many similarities between this pattern of self-justification and the traditional Judeo-Christian understanding of sin. He likes Langdon Gilkey's description of sin:

---

[34]Ibid., p. 38.

This then is the religious meaning of sin, far different from the usual meaning given it by the legalist mentality. Sin may be defined as an ultimate religious devotion to a finite interest; it is an overriding loyalty or concern for the self, its existence and its prestige, or for the existence and prestige of a group. From this deeper sin, that is, from this inordinate love of the self and its own, stem the moral evils of indifference, injustice, prejudice, and cruelty to one's neighbor, and the other destructive patterns of action that we call "sins."[35]

This inordinate self-love and preoccupation with the self is a form of idolatry. This idolatry, in turn, sets up patterns of self-deception designed to maintain a positive image of the self even if it involves dishonesty, bias and prejudice. We simply don't see ourselves as we really are. Our problem is not low self-esteem. Augustine was right about pride.

Many neo-Freudian and humanistic psychotherapists will, of course, stubbornly disagree. For them, when persons get to know themselves at a deep level, which necessitates a safe and empathic atmosphere, self-bias will fade because they will once again connect with who they truly are. They will drop their self-defenses. As the fear and estrangement, out of which they created these fictions about themselves, dissolve, they will no longer overestimate their own worth. Put differently, pride is not the primary problem.

SOCIAL CRITIQUES OF SELF-CENTEREDNESS

Cultural historian Christopher Lasch, in examining many of the social hopes of the 1960s, believes that a cynicism about genuine social change became apparent in the 1970s. As a consequence, our culture took a drastic turn inward.[36] Lasch indicts American culture as narcissistic and argues that we have lost a sense of historical continuity. Disenchanted with the possibilities of social renewal, we've embraced the maddening personal growth industry. A sense of historical rootedness in a process larger than ourselves is sacrificed.[37] The isolated, separated individual cut off from the past and unconcerned with the future is epidemic in American narcissism. An un-

---

[35]Langdon Gilkey, *Shantung Compound* (New York: Harper & Row, 1966), pp. 232-33.
[36]Christopher Lasch, *The Culture of Narcissism* (New York: W. W. Norton, 1979), pp. 3-30.
[37]Ibid., pp. 3-7.

derlying feeling that history begins with me permeates our mindset. Skepticism about the wisdom of the past and a lack of responsibility toward the future are central features of American culture. Personal experience is elevated as the only criterion for truth. This new consciousness of the self causes people to retreat from political and social involvement. Mental health is understood as renouncing all inhibitions and indulging all desires. This is a far cry from Freud's far more modest goal of therapy—to love and to work. The new brand of narcissism differs from the kind of rugged individualism in America's nineteenth-century transcendentalists such as Emerson and Thoreau. Unlike the rugged individualists who stand on their own, narcissists need a constant audience to reflect back an exaggerated self. Narcissists depend on others to validate their self-esteem. The individualists of the nineteenth century aim to conquer the wilderness, which happens to be *outside* the self.

Thus, says Lasch, therapy has become a new religion that feeds the "awareness worshippers." Two things, in particular, have ushered in the replacement of religion by therapy. One is simply the decline of religious commitment in the nineteenth and twentieth centuries. The other is the inflation of Freud, which has turned therapists into secular priests. In a fascinating article entitled "The Sacrifice of Freud," Lasch has argued that today's pop therapies have sacrificed Freud's passion for truth, honesty and objectivity.[38] Instead, an ever-expanding, joyful self is the new object of devotion.

Transforming therapy into religion misses a very important point: pop therapies are antireligious. Lasch correctly reminds us that religion tries to bring us into the context of our meaning in the overall scheme of things, that is, how we fit into a puzzle much greater than the isolated self. It seeks an all-encompassing interpretation of reality as a whole. According to Lasch, therapy, on the other hand, often wants to reduce reality to individual awareness. Therapy is unequipped to handle questions about ultimate meaning, purpose, the direction of the cosmos and so on.

Lasch makes a crucial distinction between the existentialist understanding of "authenticity" and the self-indulgence of narcissism. Existentialism's key insights into the self (from Kierkegaard to Sartre) all indicate a certain

---

[38]Lasch, "Sacrificing Freud," *New York Times Magazine,* February 22, 1976, p. 11.

critical stance that looks at the self without drowning in it. By contrast, the popularity of "confessional" literature reflects a preference for narcissistic self-exposure over insight.

Edwin Schur is another social critic who doesn't think very highly of our "awareness culture."[39] Schur believes that people are being led to believe that the origins of all their problems reside within their own psyches. The possibility of social change is "cooled out" as individuals are "therapized," and hence the status quo remains the same.[40] Schur is more concerned with the assumptions underlying the awareness craze than with the therapies themselves. This invitation for people to take responsibility for everything in their lives blinds them to the political and institutional powers around them. It encourages solipsistic inattention to those very structures that oppress. Individuals thus interiorize socioeconomic problems. The isolated "self" is viewed as an endless resource of problem-solving ability. Counseling thus serves a very important function: It cools out anger and rage over socioeconomic injustice. Instead of marching, we're talking about our childhoods. Thus, therapy functions as a tool of the status quo. Clients are told that they can "control" the problem by "choosing" to not be upset by it.

Schur tells us much about how the journey into self is a retreat from social involvement. However, he needs to realize also that social activism can be a retreat from the frightening inner world. Lasch, for one, criticizes him for setting up an unrealistic dichotomy between "personal" and "social" issues.[41] A good example of this retreat from inner issues is the social activism in the sixties when the death-of-God movement was so popular. Lacking a theological object of devotion, many seminarians and clergy hungered for something in which they could place their loyalty. The civil rights movement provided such an opportunity. Social activism, although very important, became, at least for some, a way of running away from a crisis of faith.

Schur's critique of psychotherapy is very similar to Marx's critique of religion.[42] Marx was frustrated with religion because he thought it was an ob-

---

[39]Edwin Schur, *The Awareness Trap: Self-Absorption Instead of Social Change* (New York: McGraw-Hill, 1976).

[40]Ibid.

[41]Lasch, *Culture of Narcissism*, pp. 25-27.

[42]Terry D. Cooper, "Karl Marx and Group Therapy: An Old Warning About a New Phenomenon," *Counseling and Values* 29, no. 1 (1984): 22-26.

stacle to social change. It keeps people preoccupied with an *afterlife* and, hence, decreases an interest in this world. In a similar manner, psychotherapy can be obsessed with an *innerlife*. Thus, therapy, like religion, maintains the status quo.

Cultural historian Jackson Lears makes a similar argument in his discussion of the "cult of experience" so epidemic in contemporary American life.[43] He argues that amid spiritual confusion, intense experience can become an end in itself. Unable to find larger meanings outside the self, Americans often become what Lears frequently calls "enmeshed in morbid self-consciousness."[44] By exalting "authentic experience" as an end in itself, American culture has moved from the nineteenth-century concern with salvation to the twentieth-century preoccupation with personal fulfillment. This highly exaggerates the significance of the self.

Psychology watchdog and social critic Martin Gross, in his bitingly critical *The Psychological Society*, argues that the new psychology has led us to believe there would be no failure, no unhappiness, no crime and no malevolence if we could just "adjust" our psyches.[45] He argues that the new psychology has elevated "adjustment" to a metaphysical condition. But instead of providing a greater sense of stability, this preoccupation has led to greater anxiety and insecurity. The term *sick* has rendered the traditional notion of sin obsolete.

Gross, unlike Lasch, also includes Freud in the development of our psychotherapeutic intoxication. In fact, perhaps his most interesting thesis is that believers in the religion of the hidden psyche are always looking for the "true person" who peeks through the unconscious every now and then. Our unconscious only becomes clear when we speak to a therapist-priest, who helps us with this revelation. In this religion of the unconscious, our conscious mind is a "second class being," a puppet controlled by the unconscious. We can determine our present and future *only* if we learn the mysteries of psychology. Like a primitive witch doctor, the therapist offers to help us for power and money. Gross likes Jerome Frank's comment that the mental

---

[43]T. J. Jackson Lears, *No Place for Grace: Antimodernism and the Transformation of American Culture, 1880-1920* (Chicago: University of Chicago Press, 1994).

[44]Ibid.

[45]Martin Gross, *The Psychological Society* (New York: Simon & Schuster, 1978).

health industry creates its own customers.[46] And like Lasch, Gross insists that our psychological society is not truly individualist, but self-absorbed.

Wendy Kaminer is another recent social critic of how psychotherapy, and particularly the recovery movement, has led individuals down an unfortunate path of navel-gazing.[47] Ironically, this self-absorption has deepened a sense of powerlessness and the maintenance of the status quo. Incidentally, Kaminer is not particularly critical of Alcoholics Anonymous, but she thinks this valuable recovery program has been hijacked to deal with a variety of emotional problems for which it was never well suited. For instance, she despises the word *codependent*. Her book *I'm Dysfunctional, You're Dysfunctional* contains a vicious indictment of an American culture that is more concerned with "getting in touch with its inner child" than getting in touch with their representatives in Congress.[48] For Kaminer, it's dangerous to put our faith in self-help experts. Further, the ever-expanding definitions of *addiction* and *abuse* encourage our preoccupation with victimization. As a result, we stay imprisoned within the confines of "self-exploration." Again, note the irony. While becoming more and more intoxicated with "self," we are actually conforming to covertly authoritarian self-help experts. Why? Because even though a self-absorbed culture may *seem* to encourage individuals to find their own answers, they really rely on a mystique of expertise. They encourage people to look outside themselves for standardized instructions. Like Lasch's narcissistic culture, Kaminer's self-help movement does not really seek rugged individuality.

Kaminer's theme is similar to that of social critic Charles Sykes's *A Nation of Victims: The Decay of American Culture*. Sykes describes the marketing tools of our self-preoccupied culture: "It defines as symptoms traits that are not exceptionally unusual, creates anxiety about them, and promises help. That formula, repeated over and over, is the mark of the therapeutic culture . . . and the foundation of the addiction-recovery industry."[49] Sykes also criticizes modern culture for taking age-old dilemmas and turning them into

---

[46]Jerome Frank, cited in Gross, *Psychological Society*, p. 16.

[47]Wendy Kaminer, *I'm Dysfunctional, You're Dysfunctional: The Recovery Movement and Other Self-Help Fashions* (New York: Vintage, 1993).

[48]Ibid.

[49]Charles Sykes, *A Nation of Victims: The Decline of American Culture* (New York: St. Martin's Press, 1992).

"psychological problems" that can be solved. Again, "experts" create a need for their own product. And because they connect rationality with denial, mental health gurus are able to dodge any rational challenges.

Lasch, Schur, Lears, Gross and Kaminer all believe we are entirely too focused on ourselves. Many other critiques of American culture charge essentially the same indictment against our self-absorption. This celebration and exaltation of the self turns us away from important realities which are larger than the autonomous ego. Self-exaltation distorts a social, historical and cosmic perspective of our own significance as persons.

ROGERS AND NIEBUHR AS REPRESENTATIVES OF THE DEBATE

The controversy between an overvalued and undervalued self came to a very interesting crossroads when Carl Rogers was asked to review Reinhold Niebuhr's *The Self and the Dramas of History* for the *The Chicago Theological Seminary Register* in 1956. The piece was then picked up, along with respondents' commentary, by *Pastoral Psychology,* and most recently published in *Carl Rogers—Dialogues.*[50] Although written nearly a half-century ago, the issues raised in this discussion are just as relevant today. This is an extremely important "meeting of minds" because it brought to light the conflict between one of the greatest twentieth-century commentators on the "overvalued self" (Niebuhr) and perhaps the greatest twentieth-century spokesperson for the "undervalued self" (Rogers). Representing the Augustinian tradition, Niebuhr, who has profoundly influenced social ethicists, politicians and clergy, opposes the leader of humanistic psychology, the person who has probably influenced the practice of psychological counseling more than any American in the past century. Many students in theological schools, and pastoral counseling training programs in particular, have been heavily influenced by *both* these thinkers. Even when the influence is not direct, it is hard to discuss modern understandings of self-deceit or sin without Niebuhr lurking in the back-

---

[50]Carl R. Rogers, "Reinhold Niebuhr's *The Self and the Dramas of History,*" *The Chicago Theological Seminary Register*, no. 1 (January 1956); reprinted in *Carl Rogers—Dialogues: Conversations with Martin Buber, Paul Tillich, B. F. Skinner, Gregory Bateson, Michael Polanyi, Rollo May, and Others,* ed. Howard Kirschenbaum and Valerie Land Henderson (Boston: Houghton Mifflin, 1989). References are to the Kirschenbaum and Henderson reprint.

ground. Furthermore, Carl Rogers's work, while not always studied directly, undergirds nearly any counselor education training program in America. Many of us interested in *both* Christian theology and psychotherapy have gotten a healthy dose of Niebuhr on the human condition, only to be introduced to Rogers's opposing position in counseling. The question quickly becomes, How does "sin" fit in with "'self-actualization"?

Rogers expressed agreement with much in Niebuhr's work. His central problem with Niebuhr's analysis, as we can clearly guess, concerned Niebuhr's insistence on the primacy of pride and inordinate self-love in humans. Rogers voices his disagreement well:

> It is in his conception of the basic deficiency of the individual self that I find my experience utterly at variance. He is quite clear that the "original sin" is self-love, pretension, claiming too much, grasping after self-realization. I read such words and try to imagine the experience out of which they have grown. I have dealt with maladjusted and troubled individuals, in the intimate personal relationship of psychotherapy, for more than a quarter of a century. This has not been perhaps fully representative of the whole community, but neither has it been unrepresentative. And, if I were to search for the central core of difficulty in people as I have come to know them, it is that in the great majority of cases they despise themselves, regard themselves as worthless and unlovable. To be sure, in some cases this is covered by pretension, and in nearly all these feelings are covered by a facade. But I could not differ more deeply from the notion that self-love is the fundamental and pervasive "sin."[51]

Based on his own experience in psychotherapy, clinical research and observations of people, Rogers is definitely convinced that Niebuhrian pride is never the primary problem. The undervaluing of self is what needs to be healed. This is accomplished through an accepting, empathic relationship in which a person is offered unconditional positive regard, or at least as close to unconditional positive regard as we humans are capable. Rogers goes on to describe this type of relationship and its effects:

---

[51]Ibid., pp. 210-11.

Actually it is only in the experience of a relationship in which he is loved (something very close, I believe, to the theologian's *agape*) that the individual can begin to feel a dawning respect for, acceptance of, and, finally, even a fondness for himself. It is thus that he can begin to feel love and tenderness for others. It is thus that he can begin to realize himself and to reorganize himself and his behavior to move in the direction of becoming the more socialized self he would like to be. I believe that only if one views individuals on the most superficial or external basis are they seen as being primarily the victims of self-love. When seen from the inside, that is far from being their disease. At least so it seems to me.[52]

Another way of framing this issue asks, do we human beings do destructive things to others out of a sense of strength or weakness?

REENACTMENT OF THE PELAGIAN CONTROVERSY

An interesting question lurking beneath this inquiry is whether or not this disagreement between Niebuhr (representing the Augustinian tradition) and Rogers represents another version of the ongoing Pelagian controversy. As a matter of fact, in his discussion of Rogers's review of Niebuhr's *Self and the Dramas of History,* Walter Horton makes a very interesting observation:

Carl Rogers takes such an "accepting" and permissive attitude toward his counselees that it appears to him as though their nature were fundamentally wholesome, needing only to be released from shackling external bonds in order to heal and save itself by its own internal powers. This at least leans in the direction of Pelagian self-salvation. Reinhold Niebuhr lays such stress upon the essential helplessness of man, and his utter dependence upon divine grace, fears complacency so like the very devil, that he can cry, "Cursed be the man that putteth his trust in man!" Could any view be more opposed to Pelagian optimism than this Augustinian pessimism?[53]

---

[52]Ibid., p. 211.

[53]Walter Horton, "Reinhold Niebuhr and Carl R. Rogers: A Discussion by Bernard M. Loomer, Walter Horton, and Hans Hofmann," in *Carl Rogers—Dialogues,* ed. Howard Kirschenbaum and Valerie Land Henderson (Boston: Houghton Mifflin, 1989), p. 219.

In reading this comment, Rogers, who was asked to respond to his respondents, humorously remarked, "I even found it interesting to learn that I am seen as a Pelagian. It is useful to know the labels for one's heresies."[54]

This idea that the Rogers-Niebuhr dispute in some way recycles the Pelagian controversy is worth pursuing. Pelagius, a highly controversial fifth-century monk, occupied most of Augustine's energies in the later part of Augustine's life. Pelagius held that we come into this world morally neutral and are not the carriers of Augustinian "original sin."[55] While Augustine argued that Adam's sin was passed down to us thorough the mechanism of sexual intercourse, Pelagius believed that Adam's sin affected Adam only. Furthermore, Augustine's notion of original guilt, that we somehow all participated in Adam's sin, was, for Pelagius, ridiculous. Adam set a bad example, which means that after his fall, we have to serve God in a hostile, nonsupportive environment. This sinful environment makes obedience tough, but not impossible. The power of self-determination is crucial, and it can be strengthened through pious practices. The world around us may be full of corruption, but we as individuals are not.

As a fifth-century monk, Pelagius was shocked by the moral laxity of his time.[56] He encouraged a stricter asceticism. He emphasized human freedom to do good works, apart from God's supernatural grace. Why? Because we have already been equipped with the grace necessary to obey the commandments of God. This is the grace of our nature, a reliance on our God-given capacities.

Human freedom necessitates the capacity for good or evil; hypothetically, humans *must* be able to live above sin. God has endowed humanity with the gift of free will, which is a form of natural grace. The capacity for goodness and the inborn ability to actualize this goodness resides within each of us, apart from any appeal to supernatural grace. Put simply, we have the equipment intact, but the desire to use it is completely *our* responsibility. We don't need external help in fulfilling our inherent potential. Grace is not necessary to heal

---

[54]Carl Rogers, "Concluding Comment," in *Carl Rogers—Dialogues,* ed. Howard Kirschenbaum and Valerie Land Henderson (Boston: Houghton Mifflin, 1989), p. 223.

[55]Pelagius, "Letter to Demetrius," in *Theological Anthropology,* ed. and trans. J. Patout Burns (Philadelphia: Fortress, 1981). For an excellent account of Pelagius's thought, see Robert F. Evans, *Pelagius: Inquiries and Reappraisals* (New York: Seabury Press, 1968).

[56]Pelagius, "Letter to Demetrius."

human nature because human nature is not sick. There is nothing intrinsically wrong with us. We are not depraved creatures with broken wills as Augustine argued. The first foundation for a spiritual life, therefore, is to recognize our strength. Pelagian natural integrity resembles the Rogerian self-actualizing tendency. Historical theologian Stephen Duffy points out that Pelagius was shocked by the loose living of the Roman Christians and that a *negative anthropology only made matters worse:* "To hold that people could not help sinning seemed to Pelagius demeaning to humans and an insult to their Creator."[57]

Duffy goes on to say that Pelagius probably did *not* see his own perspective as "optimistic." Moreover, there *is* a sense in which Pelagius had a notion of original sin, though it's not inherited:

> It must be noted, however, that Pelagius probably would not think his an excessively optimistic view of the human condition. He sees a cumulative intensification of the grip of evil upon the human race and upon the individual's capacity to avoid sin. Individual acts of sin snowball into social sin, thus people find themselves enslaved by sinful habits and customs and surrounded by bad examples. In this sense, one might almost claim that Pelagius ultimately did have a doctrine of original sin, because sin as social habit and custom infects us from childhood and imposes a kind of necessity of sinning, even for one who begins the course free of inherited sin. In fact, habit has such a gridlock on humanity that the Law was rendered powerless to liberate us and had to be replaced by the Law of Christ. Humans are responsible for this state of affairs; nearly all contribute to the fund of evil social habits.[58]

Rogers too, as we shall later see, does *not* believe his view of the human condition to be overly optimistic. In fact, he describes the "fall into self-alienation" as practically inevitable. He calls this discrepancy between our actual experience and our self-awareness "incongruence." This estrangement from ourselves leads us toward destructive (sinful) behavior.

Augustine, of course, had a very different view of humanity's fall. In the Garden of Eden, Adam and Eve were in a state of righteousness and friend-

---

[57]Stephen J. Duffy, *The Dynamics of Grace: Perspectives in Theological Anthropology* (Collegeville, Minn.: Michael Glazier, 1993), p. 85.
[58]Ibid., p. 88.

ship with God. They were immune from physical illness and death, pos-
sessed exceptional intellectual gifts and had nonpassionate, non-
"animalistic" sex, Augustine writes. They were free. While the inability to
sin *(non posse pecare)* was not part of their makeup, they did have the ability
not to sin *(posse non pecare)*. Endowed with an inclination to virtue, their lives
were perfectly ordered. The body was subject to the soul, the desires were
subject to reason and will, and the will to God. Nothing impeded the love
of God.

But pride, the desire to be their own God, moved them to distort what
God had made. The first sin, for Augustine, was almost unimaginable, because Adam and Eve were free unequivocally. There was absolutely no reason for it. Its reprehensible nature changed the human condition.

For Augustine, it is absolutely necessary that God's Spirit recreate the
fallen will and retrieve its ability to love God first, thus ordering our lives.
For Pelagius, on the other hand, we have our minds, the capacity to choose
right from wrong, the law and the example of Jesus. What more do we
need? He believed that Augustine's notion that only God can work good in
us undercuts the very possibility of morality.

From 412 until his death in 430, Augustine attempted to eliminate the
errors of Pelagianism. To him its central error was profoundly dangerous:
the works-righteousness monk utterly minimized the significance of divine
grace. Pelagius insisted on the human ability to keep God's commandments.
Since God had provided this capacity in creation, no "extra assistance" was
needed. This view did not take seriously the plight of human helplessness;
it eliminated original sin and therefore reduced the salvific work of Christ.
The end result of Pelagian optimism, for Augustine, was the same sort of
pride exhibited by both Satan and Adam.

The Pelagian controversy marches on and on. The issues raised by this
conflict reappeared in the Protestant Reformation, then later created a division between the Jansenists and the Jesuits in the seventeenth century. It
has prevailed in various concerns within twentieth-century theology. The
conflict does not seem to go away because it involves fundamentally different views of human potential. The Augustinian view does not seem far
from Freudian pessimism; the Pelagian view is more optimistic about our
created nature.

While a fifth-century monk and a twentieth-century psychotherapist may seem to have little in common, I find some of the parallels between Pelagius and Rogers fascinating.

Pelagius	Rogers
Denounces original sin; human beings are not "oriented" toward sin.	Denounces Freudian pessimism about human nature's inherent destructive tendencies.
Acknowledges the collective power of habit.	Acknowledges the power of "conditions of worth" leading to incongruence.
Defines sin as violating our created nature.	Defines incongruence as violating the organismic growth tendency.
Uses references to "holy men" in the Hebrew Bible, i.e., Job.	Supports Maslow's reference of self-actualizing people.
Argues that the probability of sin arises from external pressures.	Argues that the probability of incongruence arises from social expectations.
Moves away from Augustinian predestination.	Moves away from Freudian intrapsychic pessimism.
Claims that our original nature is "graced" and can be trusted.	Claims that our organismic tendency moves in a healthy direction.
Says the fall has not disturbed our created potential.	Says there is an undeniable, innate actualizing tendency.
Holds that nothing in human nature needs to be "fixed."	Holds that the human organism is completely trustworthy.
Argues that our desires are not disordered.	Argues that our instincts are not dangerous.

Despite these similarities, on one central issue the Pelagian position and the Rogerian position markedly differ. Contrary to popular criticism, Rogers does *not* believe that we can "save ourselves." While we are born with an inherent actualizing tendency, once we fall into distorted awareness, acceptance (grace) must be mediated to us. Self-acceptance and the healing of our self-estrangement comes as a result of *being* accepted and understood, and not from our own heroic efforts to accept ourselves. Healing is relational, not individual.

THE LARGER ISSUE: SIN AND SELF-ACCEPTANCE

There is a larger issue at stake here than whether a theological anthropologist such as Niebuhr can find a point of contact with a humanistic psychologist such as Rogers. The deeper issue is how we relate an emphasis on prideful self-assertion and grandiosity with a focus on the underdeveloped self. How can we talk, in the same breath, about prideful sin and low self-esteem? Can we meaningfully appropriate insights from the Augustinian-Niebuhrian tradition as well as an alternative perspective that identifies o ur problem as undervaluing ourselves? Further, does "pride" or rebellious self-assertion have a monopoly on our understanding of sin, or do we need to look at other attitudes and forms of behavior to form a more comprehensive picture of human estrangement?

Initially, the prospect of comparing a traditional Christian view of sin with the notion of self-actualization may seem like quite a challenge. In my efforts, I must not in any way minimize the differences. Yet it is my hope that a greater understanding can emerge from examining this tension. The challenge will be to show that *both* the Augustinian emphasis on pride and the humanistic emphasis on low self-esteem, however different, have something extremely important to say about the human condition.

Before any sort of integration of positions can be offered, however, we must clearly understand the polar opposition and explanatory power of both the overvalued-self perspective, as well as the undervalued-self thesis. We will first turn to the self-exaltation position, the traditional Augustinian argument, which has been richly illuminated by Reinhold Niebuhr.

PRIDE AS THE
PRIMARY PROBLEM

Thus evil in its most developed form is always a good which imagines itself, or pretends to be, better than it is.
REINHOLD NIEBUHR

Most people influenced by the Judeo-Christian tradition, particularly in the Western world, have been introduced to the idea that pride is their primary problem. This position, rooted in Paul's epistles and especially developed in the writings of Augustine, has been taken for granted throughout much of Christian theology's reflection on the human condition.

One of the most comprehensive restatements of this position can be found in the work of twentieth-century theologian and ethicist Reinhold Niebuhr. Particularly in his Gifford lectures, *The Nature and Destiny of Man*, we see Niebuhr insightfully resurrecting Augustinian pride as humanity's major culprit.[1] In describing Niebuhr's work, John Raines comments, "Not since Augustine's *City of God* have we had such a sustained and brilliant analysis of the political and social effects of man's inflated self-love."[2]

Niebuhr, with the possible exception of Jonathan Edwards, is often considered the most influential theologian in America's history. Born in Wright

---

[1]Reinhold Niebuhr, *The Nature and Destiny of Man*, vol. 1 (New York: Charles Scribner's, 1964).
[2]John Raines, "Sin as Pride and Sin as Sloth," *Christianity and Crisis*, February 3, 1969, p. 5.

City, Missouri, Niebuhr followed in the footsteps of his father, a minister in the Evangelical Synod of North America. The Evangelical Synod united with the Reformed Church in 1934, then later joined the Congregationalists to form the United Church of Christ. Niebuhr's father was heavily influenced by the great German historical theologian Adolf von Harnack. For Harnack, the heart of religion lies in its ethical principles of love and brotherhood, along with a very optimistic assessment of the human condition. Niebuhr would later hang on to this emphasis on ethical principles while denying the optimistic appraisal of the human condition.

As Harold Vanderpool puts it, Protestant liberalism and the social gospel movement were Niebuhr's "theological parents."[3] Professor Douglas Clyde Macintosh, at Yale Divinity School, further influenced Niebuhr in Protestant liberalism. The emphasis on the "social gospel" also pushed Niebuhr away from individualistic concern with personal salvation toward a broader social concern for the problems of the world. Niebuhr, even until the end of his life, hated a preoccupation with personal piety *at the expense* of a concern for social issues.

As Vanderpool indicates, the social gospel movement preached that human beings come into the world morally neutral and have an innate capacity to be altruistic.[4] Society has the ability to move progressively toward an ideal future. For the maturing Niebuhr, this was simply another manifestation of naive Pelagianism, a belief that humanity, through its own efforts, could meet divine standards of love and universal brotherhood. Later, Niebuhr radically rejected the idea that a scientific analysis of our social ills, combined with a good intention to clean them up, would make injustice go away. He grew to believe that the social gospel movement was based on an overconfidence in both humanity's rationality and goodness.

After having attended Yale, Niebuhr left at twenty-three to become a pastor in Detroit. This was shortly after the start of World War I. His reputation quickly grew as he spoke out on social issues and accused Henry Ford of social irresponsibility for opposing worker benefits such as unemploy-

---

[3]Harold Vanderpool, "Reinhold Niebuhr: Religion Fosters Social Criticism and Promotes Social Justice," in *Critical Issues in Modern Religion,* by Roger Johnson et al. (Englewood Cliffs, N.J.: Prentice-Hall, 1973).
[4]Ibid., p. 178.

ment insurance and pensions for the elderly. During the 1920s, Niebuhr contributed articles to the *Christian Century* and other national publications. All of this led to an invitation in 1928 to join the faculty of Union Theological Seminary in New York. Niebuhr took the appointment and remained there until his retirement in 1960.

ANXIETY AND PRIDE: NIEBUHRIAN THEOLOGICAL PSYCHOLOGY

The idea of a "theological" psychology may sound to some like an unfortunate hangover of a prescientific inquiry, but certainly not to Niebuhr. Niebuhr strongly believed it is impossible to have an adequate psychology (understanding of the human psyche) apart from theology (understanding of humanity's relationship to ultimate reality). Put differently, we are dependent on God for our self-understanding. The reason for this dependence is that we are "designed" for relationship, first with God and then with each other. Because we are created, we can only know ourselves most deeply in relationship to our Creator. We neither originate from ourselves nor are we the "end" of ourselves. Any psychology that makes humanity a closed system, cut off from our cosmic context, is destined to misinterpret our essential nature.

The most important thing to understand about humans, according to Niebuhr, is that we are a mixture of nature and spirit. We are a part of nature's contingencies, which means we are subject to temporality. We are finite, limited, historically and socially located. We are going to die. Yet we also have the ability to step outside of our lives and survey the meaning of our existence. We have the capacity for self-transcendence. This ability to transcend our socio-historical location and look at our lives is what it means to be created in the image of God. The *imago Dei* is not simply our capacity for rationality but instead our propensity to transcend the context of this moment. Niebuhr puts it in the following way: "In its purest form the Christian view of man regards man as a unity of God-likeness and creatureliness in which he remains a creature even in the highest spiritual dimensions of his existence and may reveal elements of the image of God even in the lowliest aspects of his natural life."[5]

---

[5]Niebuhr, *Nature and Destiny of Man,* 1:150.

This mixture of spirit and nature places us in a situation of anxiety. Being creatures confined to nature and the limitations of finitude, on the one hand, and also creatures capable of transcending and reflecting on this situation, on the other hand, produces tension. While this anxiety is not in itself a bad thing, it is the precondition for sin. It sets us up for two options: (a) trust in God or (b) trust in self. The temptation, when we experience anxiety, is to deny our creatureliness and dependence on God. We usurp God and make ourselves the center of the universe. Taking his lead from Kierkegaard, Niebuhr vividly describes this anxious condition:

> In short, man, being both free and bound, both limited and limitless, is anxious. Anxiety is the inevitable concomitant of the paradox of freedom and finiteness in which man is involved. Anxiety is the internal precondition of sin. It is the inevitable spiritual state of man, standing in the paradoxical situation of freedom and finiteness. Anxiety is the internal description of the state of temptation. It must not be identified with sin because there is always the ideal possibility that faith would purge anxiety of the tendency toward sinful self-assertion. The ideal possibility is that faith in the ultimate security of God's love would overcome all insecurities of nature and history. That is why Christian orthodoxy has consistently defined unbelief as the root of sin, or as the sin which precedes pride. It is significant that Jesus justifies his injunction, "Be not anxious," with the observation, "For your heavenly Father knoweth that ye have need of these things." The freedom from anxiety which he enjoins is a possibility only if perfect trust in divine security has been achieved. . . . No life, even the most saintly, conforms to the injunction not to be anxious.[6]

Again, for Niebuhr, nature and spirit are always linked together and cannot be separated. While they are distinguishable, they are never torn from one another. Don Browning provides an excellent statement of their connection, saying that, for Niebuhr, "nature and spirit . . . interpenetrate and mutually qualify one another. All of our natural impulses are qualified by spirit, by which he means the capacity for freedom, imagination, and self-

---

[6]Ibid., 1:183.

transcendence."[7] None of our drives and hungers are purely instinctive animal passions. "On the other hand, none of our expressions of freedom, imagination, and self-transcendence is disconnected from our biological life. Our freedom is only a freedom to orient our biology one way or the other but never to disconnect ourselves from it, totally repress it, or act forgetfully of it."[8]

"Spirit" is the capacity for freedom, imagination and self-transcendence. Contra Freud, our instincts are not raw, mechanistic inclinations determined completely by natural forces. Instead, both our freedom and imagination are part of instinctuality. Certain forms of extreme self-denial try to escape this indissoluble combination of nature and spirit. Through some form of extreme bodily denial, for instance, an attempt is made to reach "pure," almost disembodied, spirituality. Such a dichotomy, for Niebuhr, is never possible, nor is it desirable. "Spirit" can never so overcome nature that one does not experience the combination. Our bodies are not something we need to run away from in order to be "spiritual." Extreme forms of asceticism deny the only form of spirituality available to humans: an *embodied* spirituality. We cannot abort nature on our way to God.

However, for Niebuhr, the opposite is also true. We cannot escape our spiritual dimension by immersing ourselves in the delights of nature. In other words, no amount of self-indulgent hedonism can disconnect us from our self-transcending dimension. Nature and spirit are married for better or for worse. No amount of bodily denial can eliminate biology; no amount of bodily indulgence can eliminate the reaches of the spirit. Being human means being a combination of nature and spirit.

Greek thought, especially, has often tried to separate nature and spirit in such a way that perceives nature as chaotic, unregulated, irrational energy that desperately needs the realm of mind or spirit to give it form. This dualism pits chaos against order, uncontrollability against control, irrationality against reason. Put simply, "mind" has to do all the work because nature can never be counted on to realize its own limits or employ any self-control.

For Niebuhr, this dualism simply will not work. Nature should not be

---

[7]Don Browning, *Religious Thought and the Modern Psychologies* (Philadelphia: Fortress, 1987), p. 24.
[8]Ibid.

viewed as the chaotic irrational energies of life but instead as the source for
its own contribution along with spirit. Again, we are motivated by both nature and spirit. Neither can be eliminated in the name of the other.

Anxiety itself cannot be identified as sin. This would make the human
situation evil and therefore exonerate us from any responsibility for our
condition. While anxiety is built into our condition, it is not necessary that
we mishandle the anxiety and act in self-centered ways. Hypothetically, for
Niebuhr, we could rest calmly in the assurances of divine security. However,
we do not. We are not doomed in the sense that we inherit a flawed nature
that is destined to sin. However, we *are* born into a situation that produces
anxiety. Each of our lives repeats this mishandling of anxiety and distrust of
God, which was central in the Adamic story.

The crucial point here is the realization that sin does not automatically
occur as a result of our biological make-up. We are not "hard-wired" to sin.
It is not built into our true essence. Sin is not a *necessary* part of being human, even though it is an *inevitable* part of our condition. This may sound
contradictory, yet for Niebuhr, it points toward a very real paradox inherent
in our condition. Christianity is not antagonistic toward the created order.
It has no problem recognizing finite goods such as human intimacy, sexual
relatedness or even the acquisition of material goods as *genuine* goods. However, out of our anxiety, we quickly elevate those goods to the status of gods
and center our entire life around them. Valuing finite, limited things is not
corruptive; committing idolatry is. Browning points out that Niebuhr uses
the Greek word *eros* as shorthand for "all aspects of natural human striving,"
and he considers all these good. Sin does not result simply from pursuing
these goods. "It is rather the reality of anxiety and sin that distorts natural
self-regard (eros) into inordinate self-regard and a concupiscent striving to
have more than we need or, as we moderns sometimes say, to 'have it all.'"[9]
This point will be crucial later when we look at the place of self-regard in
both the overvaluing and undervaluing of our worth. For now, it is important to note that self-regard, properly maintained, is *not* something Niebuhr
asks us to abandon. Yet he tirelessly warns against the dangers of inordinate
self-regard, a preoccupation that distances us from both God and neighbor.

---

[9]Ibid., p. 26.

DIFFERENCES WITH AUGUSTINE

While Niebuhr has done a great deal to resurrect the traditional concept of "original sin," he parts company with Augustine, the doctrine's primary architect, in some ways. First, Niebuhr does not treat the Fall as an historical event in which the first couple was kicked out of the garden of innocence. There was no golden era in our collective historical past. For Augustine, of course, the pride and disobedience of the first couple provides a causal explanation for how sin entered the world. Unlike previous exegetes such as Philo and Origen who had allegorized the Genesis couple, Augustine literally explained both the origin and the sexual transmission of sin. For Niebuhr, unlike Augustine, we cannot find a historical cause of sin. Yet the Genesis allegory does indeed tell our story as well.

Augustine also provided a rather elaborate description of life before the Fall. This prefallen state, contrary to many Augustinian critics, *did* involve sexuality. However, it was a passionless sexuality, void of the brute desires that accompany fallen sexuality. Sexual activity was a calm, deliberate expression of the mind, not a captive of sinful lust.[10] Niebuhr, on the other hand, does not believe we can know anything about prefallen humanity because, once again, the Genesis story does not point toward a historical first couple. Instead, it points toward our experience in the here and now.

> The myth does not record any actions of Adam which were sinless, though much is made in theology of the perfection he had before the Fall. Irenaeus, with greater realism than most theologians, observes that the period was very brief, sin following almost immediately upon his creation. Adam was sinless before he acted and sinful in his first recorded action. His sinlessness, in other words, preceded his first significant action and his sinfulness came to light in that action. This is a symbol for the whole of human history.[11]

Niebuhr affirms, however, the manner in which Augustine refuses to locate the source of sin in Adam or Eve's rebellious *behavior* when they ate the fruit. Instead, sin grew in the first couple's gradual desire to be disconnected

---

[10]Augustine, *City of God,* book 14, trans. Henry Bettenson (New York: Penguin Classics, 1972).
[11]Niebuhr, *Nature and Destiny of Man,* 1:279-80.

from their Creator and to be the center of their own world. This preceded
any rebellious activity. It was the development of pride in Adam that
prompted him to commit the act of disobedience. Put differently, the Fall
began in Adam's mind long before he ate the forbidden fruit. Eating the
fruit simply manifested an internal process of protest that had already been
going on. Augustine puts it this way:

> We can see then that the Devil would not have entrapped man by the
> obvious and open sin of doing what God had forbidden, had not man
> already started to please himself. That is why he was delighted also
> with the statement, "You will be like gods." In fact, they would have
> been better able to be like gods if they had in obedience adhered to
> the supreme and real ground of their being, if they had not in pride
> made themselves their own ground. . . . This then, is the original evil:
> man regards himself as his own light, and turns away from that light
> which would make man himself a light if he would set his heart on it.
> This evil came first, in secret, and the result was the other evil, which
> was committed in the open. For what the Bible says is true: "Before a
> fall the mind is exalted; before honor it is humbled" (Proverbs 18:12).
> The fall that happens in secret inevitably precedes the fall that happens
> in broad daylight, though the former is not recognized as fall. Does
> anyone think of exaltation as a fall, even though the falling away was
> already there, in the desertion of the Most High? On the other hand,
> no one could fail to see that there is a fall when there is an obvious
> and unmistakable transgression of a commandment.[12]

Thus, for Augustine, the disobedience of the first couple was an external
demonstration of an internal process that had been gradually developing.
On this point, Niebuhr is thoroughly Augustinian.

He disagrees with Augustine, however, on the extent of the damage done
by original sin. For Augustine, we are so infected by Adam's sin that grace
is necessary for us to even know we are sinners. Niebuhr believes that a
sense of obligation, a desire for forgiveness and a sense of what the nineteenth-century theologian Schleiermacher called "absolute dependence"

---

[12]Augustine, *City of God*, p. 573.

remain as part of our nature, in spite of sin.[13] Somehow we know, at a deep level, that things are not the way they were intended to be. Niebuhr understands this sense of obligation and "uneasy conscience" as an aspect of general, not special, revelation.

The major point of the notion of original sin, for Niebuhr, is to remind us that we are unable, by our own efforts, to heal our brokenness with God and neighbor. Ted Peters provides a very helpful comment concerning the Niebuhrian purpose of the idea of original sin: "To make this point it is not necessary to posit the historicity of the Garden of Eden or to employ the disease metaphor wherein we inherit a predisposition of sinning. The paradise story and the concept of inherited sin are the dressing for the otherwise naked proposition that God and God alone is responsible for establishing a divine-human relationship that is salvific."[14]

The Augustinian historical-causal explanation of the transmission of sin has sometimes had a shaming, dehumanizing and psychologically abusive effect. For Augustine, no one else in the history of humanity has ever experienced the "created goodness" that Adam knew for a brief time. When Adam rebelled, all of us, even babies born in the twenty-first century, were somehow involved in that decision. This mysterious solidarity with our first ancestor sets us up not only for original sin, but for *original guilt* as well. We, too, somehow made that choice in Adam's loins. Consequently, the next logical, but deplorable, Augustinian step is to say that even infants, if unbaptized, are damned because of the taint of original sin and guilt. Thus, in this historical-causal explanation, everyone since Adam is indeed born in sin, with a kind of genetic predisposition toward evil. At one time Adam may have had "essential goodness," but that element has forever been lost to the rest of humanity.

The move from original sin to original guilt seems to have the practical, existential implication for each of us that we are created evil. We are guilty for simply existing. Yet our existence, not some allegorical existence of our first parents, is all we know. Augustine may argue that Adam's essence was created good at one time, but *our essence* begins in a flawed, defective, corrupt

[13]Niebuhr, *Nature and Destiny of Man*, 1:128-31.
[14]Ted Peters, *Playing God: Genetic Determinism and Human Freedom* (New York: Routledge, 1997), p. 88.

state. We don't simply enter a sinful world; we *are* sinful for simply showing up! Augustine may have been a champion of created goodness in his fight with the Manichaeans, but for all practical purposes, Adam's descendants are born "in evil." Embodied existence itself is sinful because we have inherited a corrupt disposition. Paul Ricoeur powerfully addresses this issue:

> The harm that has been done to souls, during the centuries of Christianity, first by literal interpretation of the story of Adam, and then by the confusion of this myth, treated as history, with later speculations, principally Augustinian, about original sin, will never be adequately told. In asking the faithful to confess belief in this mythico-speculative mass and to accept it as a self-sufficient explanation, the theologians have unduly required a *sacrificium intellectus* where what was needed was to awaken believers to a symbolic superintelligence of their actual condition.[15]

In addition, the concept of original sin, rooted in a historical-causal explanation, may have been intellectually satisfying as long as we could point toward a historical Adam and Eve and a prefallen state of perfection. However, for many Christians who hold to some form of divinely directed evolution, contemporary evolutionary science has rendered such a golden era in human history quite unlikely. A literal, historical, space-and-time Fall contradicts the way many—though not all—believers understand humanity's evolutionary history.

We might summarize Augustine's legacy on this topic this way: Augustine's brilliant but exaggerated explanation of original sin, a theory that attempted to salvage human goodness from the Gnostic idea that created existence is evil, was sabotaged by his development of original guilt. For now, the world into which each of Adam's descendants is born is indeed a Manichaean world whose very structure is evil. Niebuhr explains the ramifications of orthodoxy's making the doctrine of "original sin" into a doctrine of an "inherited corruption" by its "effort to extend the history of sin from its origin through successive generations of mankind." While theologians could never identify its nature precisely, it was usually linked with sex-

---

[15]Paul Ricoeur, *Symbolism of Evil* (Boston: Beacon, 1967), p. 239.

ual desire and reproduction. "If original sin is an inherited corruption, its inheritance destroys the freedom and therefore the responsibility which is basic to the conception of sin. The orthodox doctrine is therefore self-destructive."[16] Niebuhr argues that Augustine's presuppositions prevented him from solving this problem. Rather than being "an inherited corruption," original sin "is an inevitable fact of human existence, the inevitability of which is given by the nature of man's spirituality. It is true every moment of existence, but it has no history."[17]

For Niebuhr, what has been "lost" in our fall into sin (through the mishandling of anxiety and the distortion of our freedom) are the relational qualities of faith, hope and love. These three qualities are part of our created essence, but they have been greatly wounded. Without faith in the providence of God, anxiety overwhelms our freedom. Again, this overwhelming quality tempts us to seek refuge in self-sufficiency or self-mastery. Put simply, we become obsessed with controlling that which is clearly beyond our abilities to control. Second, hope is a part of faith insofar as it sees infinite possibilities in God's providential care. Without this hope, the future may indeed look like blind chance or pure caprice, each of which can trigger a paralyzing fear. And third, real community among individuals is only possible through love. But in order for this love to take place, we must be freed from the grip of anxiety. As Niebuhr puts it so well, "Without freedom from anxiety man is so enmeshed in the vicious circle of egocentricity, so concerned, about himself, that he cannot release himself for the adventure of love."[18] This point that the prison of egocentricity is built on the foundation of anxiety will be explored in more detail later in this study. For now, let us simply say that without faith in God, humanity inevitably feels anxiety. And with no trust in a providential God, we cannot get out of our self-preoccupations long enough to love.

A key Niebuhrian point emphasizes that the source of sin is not in what we do but in what we wish to be. Adam, symbolizing humanity, wanted to be more than human, to move beyond the confines of human creatureliness. He was not just presented with the possibility of disobedience. Instead,

---

[16]Reinhold Neibuhr, *An Interpretation of Christian Ethics* (San Francisco: Harper & Row, 1935), p. 55.
[17]Ibid.
[18]Niebuhr, *Nature and Destiny of Man,* 1:162.

it was the serpent's analysis of the situation that tempted him. This analysis offered Adam two important things: (a) a very attractive image of becoming Godlike, which further explained his current limitations, and (b) a promise to end the current tension between finitude and freedom. The serpent suggested that it was within Adam's power to transcend human finitude. The snake further portrayed God as jealously guarding his monopoly on the knowledge of good and evil. Without this false interpretation of the serpent there would be no temptation.

This encounter with the serpent conveys the essence of original sin, that is, the meaning of original sin is that sin was in the world before any of us made our first choice. Niebuhr suggests that while the Genesis account does not contain a developed satanology, Christian theologians have not been wrong in identifying the serpent with the devil. As Niebuhr puts it, "To believe that there is a devil is to believe that there is a principle or force of evil antecedent to any evil action."[19] The story of a cosmic fall prior to human sin is a way of symbolizing the reality that sin is present before any person makes a choice. Human beings do not create sin *ex nihilo.* Thomas Oden's comment is helpful here: "Just as the Judeo-Christian tradition has spoken of the sin of 'Adam' (mankind as a whole), so has social psychology spoken of the human predicament in terms of the social transmission of distorted forms of consciousness and ideology."[20]

So sin does not emerge from our biology, as Augustine suggested in his concept of inherited sin transmitted sexually. However, neither is it merely a social disease as Protestant liberalism taught. It cannot be blamed exclusively on outside factors, which humanity will eventually clean up. Instead, we sin out of our own existential freedom. Fair social conditions, racial equality, the abolition of sexism and healthy parenting are all wonderful goals. Yet they will not rid us of the potential for sin because they cannot rid us of the problem of anxiety in the face of freedom.

Finally, Niebuhr—and the whole biblical tradition, he believes—moves away from the generic question about the origin of evil and moves instead to the existential question, how did each of us come to reject our bond with

---

[19]Ibid., 1:180.
[20]Thomas Oden, *The Structure of Awareness* (Nashville: Abingdon, 1969), pp. 72-73.

God? Augustine's elaborate theory of the origins of sin takes a back seat to the existential question of our own sin. As Kierkegaard says, "How sin came into the world, each man understands solely by himself."[21] We must ask about our *own* sin, not about a scientific understanding of how sin began.

> So when the single individual is stupid enough to inquire about sin as if it were something foreign to him, he only asks as a fool, for either he does not know at all what the question is about, and thus cannot come to know it, or he knows it and understands it, and also knows that no science can explain it to him.[22]

In other words, we cannot step outside of our own condition and investigate the origins of egoistic self-deception as if that investigation itself is untainted by our condition. The biblical tradition feels no imperative to explain the precise reason our condition came about. Instead, it begins with the realism of *what is*. Sin is first and foremost an existential problem.

NIEBUHR AND FREUD: THE DECEPTIVE NATURE OF SIN

Niebuhr found much value in the work of Freud as he attempted to clarify the deceitful nature of human sin. While he parts company with some of Freud's ideas, Niebuhr has great respect for Freud's realistic conception of the human psyche. This appreciation relates especially to the manner in which Freud blows the whistle on the proud accomplishments of the Enlightenment.

While Enlightenment philosophies are diverse, the unifying element is a positive assessment of human potential. Some perspectives elevate reason as the primary guide of human life. For others, nature herself offers the most promise. The underlying philosophical assumption is that any tendency toward evil within us can be eliminated. From such a perspective, the idea of "original sin" seems hopelessly outdated.

Yet Freud reconstructed an older pessimism about human nature using modern, scientific language. His discussion of the inevitability of egoistic

---

[21]Søren Kierkegaard, *The Concept of Anxiety,* trans. Reidar Thomte (Princeton, N.J.: Princeton University Press, 1980), p. 51.
[22]Ibid., p. 50.

corruption breathed new life into the outmoded notion of sin.

Freud's tripartite theory of the person (id, ego, superego)[23] challenged any form of simple dualism; we are much more complicated than that. The older mind-body dualism contains a naive assumption—namely, that if the mind is sufficiently awakened, it will control the rest of the psyche and regulate all bodily impulses. Reason typically functions as savior of the psyche, as it redeems and orders human impulses on a guided course.

It is very difficult to estimate how much the Freudian view of rationality upset centuries of calm confidence in reason's potential. Freud relentlessly insisted that reason itself is often the tool of more primitive impulses. Behavior is justified through endless rationalizations. The conscious ego, proud of its "control" over the psyche, often does not have a clue what is occurring beneath the surface. Unconscious factors easily sabotage the "purely rational" decisions we all make. Reason simply does not have the godlike status that many Enlightenment philosophers want it to have. Sounding much like Freud, Niebuhr says, "Reason is never completely emancipated from the particular and parochial interests of the individual and collective particular."[24]

Niebuhr believes that even in the French Enlightenment, with its emphasis on nature rather than mind, it is still the job of reason to lead us back to nature. Reason can be trusted to provide this function. Once reason has led us back to nature, however, nature can be completely trusted. Thus, the Romantic picture that became prominent envisions the natural self uncorrupted by external factors and freed from the social tyrannies that would contaminate its innocence.

Yet a Freudian conception of the human psyche challenges this simple return to the innocence of nature as much as it challenges the overconfidence in pure reason. "Nature" does not offer the unambiguous source of goodness that the Romantics want us to believe. The presumably benign survival impulse is mixed with a "pleasure impulse," a self-seeking, primitive urge that especially seeks sexual gratification. A simple laissez-faire world of libertarianism unencumbered by the intrusions of society will never work. The id, which represents this primal impulse, must be redi-

---

[23]Sigmund Freud, *The Ego and the Id,* trans. James Strachey (New York: Norton, 1962).
[24]Niebuhr, *Nature and Destiny of Man,* 1:268.

rected. The life force, or survival impulse, is far more complicated than the Romantics had ever estimated. Redemption never lies in a simple return to nature. The reason for this is that human nature itself is not singularly directed toward healthy survival and cooperation among persons. We humans have an inordinate tendency to seek pleasure, often at the cost of other human life. This is basic to our condition, and not some ill effect of the socialization process. The "pleasure principle," on which this natural impulse is based, is selfish, self-centered and concerned only with its own gratification. Without some sort of check from society, the pleasure principle will render civilization impossible. Thus, there is an inevitable, unavoidable conflict in the human organism, the battle between the id's *yes* to indulgence and the internalized *no* of society.[25]

This forms the battleground out of which human life must be lived. Both rationalism and romanticism fail to understand this unavoidable conflict. We may learn to tame this dilemma but we will never eliminate it. And for Freud, this tension will not be resolved through any vision of historical progress. It is simply part of the human condition, rooted in the biological dimension of our social existence. Put simply, these primitive instincts are not simply going to go away.

This is a crucial point because we will see this "return to nature" theme emerge again in the humanistic psychologies. The innocence of the child, still not affected by the polluting nature of society, will be raised as a model of mental health. Thus, therapy will take the form of a return to a lost innocence, a "homecoming," a reconnection with one's "inner child."[26] The assumption holds that human nature can be completely trusted to lead us in a healthy direction. In fact, psychological problems are always related to a distrust in this basic organismic trustworthiness. We need to stay out of nature's way and allow each person to be self-directing. There is no innate selfishness, self-centeredness or inordinate pleasure-seeking. Thus we need to reconnect with the vitalities of this inherent self-actualizing tendency.

---

[25]Freud, *Ego and the Id*.

[26]Though this language is perhaps most associated with the work of John Bradshaw, the elevation of childlike awareness as a criteria for mental health is widespread in humanistic psychology, on which Bradshaw leans heavily. For an interesting review, see Thomas F. Finger, *Self, Earth and Society* (Downers Grove, Ill.: InterVarsity Press, 1997), esp. chap. 2.

But for Freud, as Thomas Finger reminds us, "the self is not nearly so much discovered as it is created and recreated amid conflicting pressures."[27] There is no innate, deeper self or pregiven potential in harmony with our instincts.

A Freudian influence on Niebuhr can be seen in Niebuhr's discussion of the intricate self-deceptions of which pride is capable.[28] Human beings love themselves inordinately. Since finite existence does not deserve such worship, it is necessary for the mind to engage in endless maneuvers to trick itself. This mechanism of deception is not pure ignorance, nor is it simple dishonesty. Instead, pride employs concealment and fog as its tools. Again, the founder of psychoanalysis offers Niebuhr a powerful, secular version of original sin. Consistently, Niebuhr is attracted more to Freudian pessimism than to any sort of romanticized image of human potential.

Sin does not want to be exposed. It is intricately subtle, clever and tricky, always hiding just outside of conscious awareness. This is the case for the individual, and especially for society. Collective pride blinds individual adherents to its own idolatries. Group pride achieves an authority over the individual and demands conformity. For Niebuhr, once again, groups are always more dangerous than individuals. "The pride of nations consists in the tendency to make unconditioned claims for their conditioned values."[29] Nazi Germany is a perfect example of this profound Niebuhrian truth.

While incorporating some of Freud's insights, Niebuhr clearly rejects Freud's notion of a mechanistic universe. For Freud, of course, there is nothing outside or beyond the natural realm. Niebuhr differs with Freud in that he believes both nature and spirit motivate and order our lives. For Niebuhr, it is wrong to view our "animal natures" as simply the raw, instinctual, primitive urges and appetites of the id. The natural part of our created condition does not inordinately yearn for pleasure-seeking without limits or any form of order. Instead, even our "lower" nature, in its undistorted form, has some degree of self-regulation apart from the impositions placed on it from reason

---

[27]Ibid., p. 38.
[28]Reinhold Niebuhr, "Human Creativity and Self-Concern in Freud's Thought," in *Freud and the Twentieth Century*, ed. Benjamin Nelson (Gloucester, Mass.: Peter Smith, 1974).
[29]Niebuhr, *Nature and Destiny of Man*, 1:213.

and culture.[30] Put in Augustinian terms, concupiscence is not our *natural* condition. Our appetites are not, in their undistorted condition, excessive.

So, as we have noted, humanity's spiritual dimension has its own energies and vitalities and does not simply borrow or transform the energies of the id. Great works of art, for instance, need not be reduced to the yearnings of our primitive instincts, which have been rechanneled into a socially acceptable form. Again, the spiritual dimension can motivate itself without the help of the id. The capacity for self-transcendence is a powerful incentive.

In addition, the dilemmas of human life do not all emerge from the unchecked instinctual life of humans. The spiritual component of the human condition (i.e., the capacity for self-transcendence) can create its own problems without any help from the "lower" realm. In fact, it is these "higher" sins (pride, greed, ambition) which Niebuhr especially likes to expose.

THE PRIMACY OF PRIDE

Niebuhr believes he has the support of biblical psychology and a strong strand of the Christian tradition when he says that pride is our most basic problem. He realizes, of course, that there is not unanimous agreement here. The classical (Greek) view of the person raises its head at times, and when it does, the primary enemies become ignorance and the passions of the body, rather than pride. However, Niebuhr believes the more consistent strand of the tradition sees the primacy of pride. Our passions are a problem when we disconnect from our source and make ourselves the center of the universe. Self-elevation precedes indulgence.

Pride has both a vertical and horizontal dimension. The vertical dimension is rebellion against God. The moral and social dimension consists of oppression of our brothers and sisters, the subordination of others to our own prideful intentions. Niebuhr identifies four types of pride. All of these can be empirically verified if we simply look at human behavior. Let's examine each of them separately.

1. Pride of power. In the pride of power, the human ego assumes a self-sufficiency and self-mastery that ignores the vicissitudes of history.[31] It in-

---

[30]Browning, *Religious Thought and the Modern Psychologies,* p. 24.
[31]Niebuhr, *Nature and Destiny of Man,* 1:188.

cludes lust for more and more power. Whether the individual or group is already in a position of authority, or whether the individual or group is seeking to eliminate its insecurity by rising to the top, the will-to-power is behind the wheel. As Niebuhr puts it, "In the one case the ego seems unconscious of the finite and determinate character of its existence. In the other case the lust for power is prompted by a darkly conscious realization of its insecurity."[32] The will-to-power does not see its weakness as it arrogantly struts its authority and power. It is ignorant of the precarious underpinnings of its boastful sense of self. This is the power of pride in its obvious manifestation. It's insecurity is eclipsed from its viewpoint. It is, quite simply, "full of itself."

But this is not the only form of prideful power. The other form of a will-to-power is drunk on the wine of its own upward climb, seeking to eliminate its weakness through the capture of more power. In a sense, it is fueled by its underlying insecurity. It must "fix" the precarious conditions of human existence by rising to the top and making itself invulnerable. This is the pride of excessive ambition. In a sense, this is a pride in the vision of what we will be. This image dangles in the future and functions as a sacred absolute. "We're on our way to the top."

In both cases the achievements of the ego are elevated to a godlike status. Whether we believe we have arrived or are still on our way, the focus is a prideful exaltation of the powerful self. Both types of the power of pride are obsessed with self and attempt to escape the limitations of finitude.

It is very important to emphasize both of these forms. Critics of Niebuhr may too quickly dismiss him for not seeing the apparent insecurity underlying most so-called pride cases. However, Niebuhr is actually quite aware of this. His point remains, however, that whether one is drunk on the glory of who one is or who one will be, the underlying dynamic is an undue focus on self, a focus that wants to end in self-adulation. The drive to eliminate all insecurity is itself a manifestation of the lust for an all-consuming power. Psychotherapy clients who want to get rid of every feeling of insecurity and be completely confident within themselves often manifest this prideful worship of the imperturbable self. They search for an inward place in which

---

[32]Ibid., 1:189.

they will feel all-powerful. The desire to fortify the ego in such a way that it is never shaken by the vicissitudes of life is a longing for total power. In a sense, it is a search for the messianic ego whose strength will provide a perfect inner kingdom.

Niebuhr is especially fond of using greed as an important example of this second form of the pride of power. "Greed is in short the expression of man's inordinate ambition to hide his insecurity in nature."[33] Greed is often the dominant manifestation of pride in a bourgeois culture. The excessive drive to find a place of comfort and security tends to forget the epitome of insecurity, death.

Furthermore, this will-to-power does not just strive to conquer nature or eliminate life's vicissitudes. Other competing egos are also perceived as a threat. Because other persons represent a threat to one's position of dominance, they must be subordinated under one's control. Security means eliminating the competition. Consequently, injustice is necessary to maintain our secure place. "The will-to-power in short involves the ego in injustice. It seeks a security beyond the limits of human finiteness and this inordinate ambition arouses fears and enmities which the world of pure nature, with its competing impulses of survival, does not know."[34]

Niebuhr is not convinced that dominant psychologies of his day go far enough in understanding the relationship between this will-to-power and the fundamental anxiety that underlies it. For instance, while Adler recognizes the will-to-power, he overly associates it with specific forms of inferiority and mistakenly believes that therapy can eliminate it.[35] While Karen Horney connects the will-to-power to a broader sense of anxiety than specific cases of inferiority, she hopes that it can be eliminated in a cooperative society.[36] For Niebuhr, both of these perspectives fall short because they do not realize that anxiety is basic to human existence. It is this inherent anxiety in our situation as self-transcending creatures that makes it impossible to "therapize" or "socialize" it away. "The truth is that man is tempted by

---

[33]Ibid., 1:191.
[34]Ibid., 1:192.
[35]Alfred Adler, *What Life Should Mean to You* (1931; reprint, New York: Capricorn, 1958).
[36]Karen Horney, *The Neurotic Personality of Our Time* (New York: W. W. Norton, 1937), pp. 240-47; Niebuhr, *Nature and Destiny of Man,* 1:192-93.

the basic insecurity of human existence to make himself doubly secure and by the insignificance of his place in the total scheme of life to prove his significance. The will-to-power is in short both a direct form and an indirect instrument of the pride which Christianity regards as sin in its quintessential form."[37]

Niebuhr reminds us that the distinction between these two forms of the will-to-power is merely provisional. Even the most secure monarch experiences the whispering voices of insecurity beneath the obvious appearance of dominance. And no position of power eliminates the fear that power could be taken away. The wealthier we are, the more we are frightened by the thought of poverty. Furthermore, the threat of death is the greatest sabotaging factor, always contaminating any sense of absolute inner security. Niebuhr suggests that perhaps this is why even the pharaohs of Egypt exhausted the resources of their domain to build the pyramids, a symbol of their immortality.[38]

> The fact that human ambitions know no limits must therefore be attributed not merely to the infinite capacities of the human imagination but to an uneasy recognition of man's finiteness, weakness and dependence, which become the more apparent the more we seek to obscure them, and which generate ultimate perils, the more immediate insecurities are eliminated. Thus man seeks to make himself God because he is betrayed by both his greatness and his weakness; and there is no level of greatness and power in which the lash of fear is not at least one strand in the whip of ambition.[39]

Thus, Niebuhr recognizes the insecurity underlying the quest for self-exaltation, yet he believes that the frantic attempt to gain security and internal power involves undue focus on self.

2. Intellectual pride. Intellectual pride is less crude than the will-to-power, but it is often connected to it. In other words, every powerful group seeks ideological justification, which it equates with divine truth.[40] Intellec-

---

[37]Niebuhr, *Nature and Destiny of Man*, 1:192.
[38]Ibid., 1:194.
[39]Ibid.
[40]Ibid.

tual insecurity, like all forms of insecurity, must be eliminated in the conviction that we have come to a final, absolute truth. Niebuhr summarizes this issue:

> All human knowledge is tainted with an "ideological" taint. It pretends to be more than it is. It is finite knowledge, gained from a particular perspective; but it pretends to be final and absolute knowledge. Exactly analogous to the cruder pride of power, the pride of intellect is derived on the one hand from ignorance of the finiteness of the human mind and on the other hand from an attempt to obscure the known conditioned character of human knowledge and the taint of self-interest in human truth.[41]

Thus, intellectual pride frequently considers itself as having the final truth, the last word, the full picture, which historically previous amateurs struggled to possess. "Each great thinker makes the same mistake, in turn, of imagining himself the final thinker."[42] Descartes, Hegel, Kant and Comte are, for Niebuhr, obvious examples of intellectual hubris. And in particular, he indicts the smug certainty of post-Enlightenment naturalistic philosophy for thinking it has "arrived." The self-congratulation so typical of modern thought betrays the dim awareness that it, too, offers merely a version of the truth from a particular historical framework. The pride of reason always forgets its place, or perhaps more accurately, forgets that it has a place in the ongoing flow of history. It does not transcend history. Yet this is what it often ignores. Believing it has roped and tied the Absolute, it is embarrassingly alienated from its own limits. It can always see those limits in other perspectives, but it is blind to its own. But for Niebuhr, this blindness does not represent an innocent ignorance. Instead, it is the avoidance of a dim awareness that one's own position, too, cannot be the final arbiter of all truth. We are all citizens of our own time.

At this point particularly, Niebuhr criticizes Marxism. Marx vividly points out the ideological taint and self-serving nature of various worldviews but fails to turn those critical guns on himself. As Niebuhr puts it,

---

[41]Ibid., 1:194-95.
[42]Ibid., 1:195.

"The proud achievement of Marxism in discovering the intellectual pride and pretension of previous cultures therefore ends in a pitiful display of the same sin."[43]

The juxtaposition of nature and spirit in us is once again the driving force for our intellectual struggles. If we were not capable of transcending our situation and reflecting on it, we would simply rest content with our immediate understanding and feel no need to claim an absolute validity for it. On the other hand, this capacity to transcend the confines of our situation tempts us to forget our concrete location and to believe we have the truth in final form. Then since we "own" this final truth, we are justified to dominate those who do not agree.

3. Pride of virtue, morality and self-righteousness. What is good for me becomes an unconditional moral value for everyone else. Moral pride is most easily recognizable in the self-righteous judgments of other persons. When we judge others by our own criteria, we often mistake our own opinions for God's standards. Someone else's nonconformity to our standards then becomes the very essence of evil. As Niebuhr puts it, "Moral pride is the pretension of finite man that his highly conditioned virtue is the final righteousness and that his very relative moral standards are absolute. Moral pride thus makes virtue the very vehicle of sin, a fact which explains why the New Testament is so critical of the righteous in comparison with 'publicans and sinners.' "[44] Niebuhr is in complete agreement with Luther's insistence that the unwillingness of the sinner to be regarded as sinner is the final form of sin.[45]

Niebuhr also holds that the sin of self-righteousness is the "final sin" not only in the subjective sense but in the objective sense as well. In other words, self-righteousness is responsible for the most serious cruelties, injustices and dehumanizing actions toward our brothers and sisters. "The whole history of racial, national, religious and other struggles is a commentary on the objective wickedness and social miseries which result from self-righteousness."[46]

4. Spiritual pride. Spiritual pride is the quintessential form of pride. Here

---

[43]Ibid., 1:197.
[44]Ibid., 1:199.
[45]Martin Luther, cited in Niebuhr, *Nature and Destiny of Man*, 1:200n.
[46]Ibid., 1:200.

we claim religious legitimation for our intolerance. This form of pride is an extension of moral pride but it grounds itself in a religious framework. In one breath, argues Niebuhr, we may claim God as our judge; in the next breath we will attempt to demonstrate how God is on our side. The intricate web of human deception allows us to turn today's humility into tomorrow's pride *about that humility*. It is the all-too-human tendency to move from "God has revealed Godself to me" to "I 'own' God's revelation." Spiritual or religious one-upmanship is, again, the epitome of pride.

When stubborn, intolerant habits of mind are sanctioned by religion, it is extremely difficult to communicate. Any therapist who has worked with a religious authoritarian understands the problem when a family member justifies his or her intolerance, stubbornness or rightness with a religious sanction. The father who cannot be approached because of his dogmatism may claim that he alone stands for God's truth in the family. Communication and the possibility of family closeness is blocked because of religiously sanctioned judgmentalism and pride. Religiously justified intolerance is the worst kind of intolerance.

WARNING ABOUT EQUATING NARCISSISM WITH NIEBUHRIAN PRIDE

Niebuhr believed that self-exaltation is a universal problem, not the particular pathology of a narcissistic personality disorder. We all participate in this dilemma. It is our common problem as human beings. Any attempt to place Niebuhr's anthropology within the confines of a specific psychological diagnosis (such as narcissism) minimizes Niebuhr's analysis. His is a theological diagnosis of all children of God, not an analysis of the much smaller segment clinically categorized as narcissists. Even the looser use of the word *narcissism* to describe the self-absorption of our "me generation" does not adequately comprehend Niebuhr's analysis. Why? Because social theorists believe that our cultural problem of narcissism has socioeconomic roots and is not "built into" the human condition. Put differently, this definition of *narcissism* sees the trend toward cultural absorption as a historical, not an ontological, problem.

Again, Niebuhr believes the problem of pride and idolatry has been around as long as human beings have had to deal with their anxieties in the face of finitude. This is not a cultural trend. It's the way things are. Niebuhr dares to speak universally and transhistorically. As we noted, he believes the Genesis story describes humanity's experience precisely because it is a story, a tale about the way we find ourselves in each historical period. Psychopathologies sometimes change from era to era, but sin remains the same. It is the ongoing saga of the Fall.

SUMMARY

These, then, are the various manifestations of pride identified by Niebuhr. The consistent undercurrent beneath them is a mismanagement of anxiety coupled with an idolatrous focus on self. Whether the pride of power, intellect, morality or spirituality, it replaces our Source, God, by self.

Niebuhr's analysis of the relationship between anxiety and self-inflation is profoundly insightful. It seems relevant to our cultural predicament, even several decades after his famous Gifford lectures. Niebuhr strongly argues that our essence as persons is in our bond with God and others. We are created for relationship. For Niebuhr, this liberates us from a frantic attempt to find satisfaction and fulfillment in ourselves. Narcissistically attempting to find fulfillment strictly from within, apart from relationship, is a trap. This is especially important to grasp in our psychological culture's emphasis on such themes as "being your own best friend" or its endless strategies for building self-esteem and self-acceptance apart from human community. Countless times individuals psychologically demonstrate Luther's great truth that we simply cannot accept, justify or "declare ourselves okay" in isolation. The self's own testimony does not mean much when it is the self who is on trial in the first place. The ability to accept oneself must first be mediated by an accepting, nonjudgmental other.

Because we are *both* nature and spirit, we humans are inevitably anxious. That anxiety, in itself, does not lead to sin or disturbed behavior. However, it does create a situation in which we inevitably, though not necessarily, move away from a calm trust in our Source and make ourselves the center of all life. This deification of self precedes problems with inordinate desire. We reject our creatureliness in a frantic effort at self-mastery. Pride, the result of not remembering our status in relationship to our Creator, can take various forms. In each of these, it is an attempt to be God.

When we fail to trust God in the midst of our anxiety and we unduly exalt self as the center of the universe, it disturbs our relationships with others and distorts ordinary human desires. These desires, which are not corrupt in themselves, easily become corrupt because of anxious self-concern. While our primary problem is not our desires but the distrust of God and the anxious exaltation of ourselves, our desires *do become* excessive and problematic once self-idolatry has begun.

But what, more specifically, is the relationship between these excessive desires and undue self-focus? What does pride have to do with the "sins of the flesh"? In today's language, what does an overvalued self have to do with addiction? Niebuhr wrote relatively little on the problem of inordinate desire (sensuality) compared to his enormous focus on pride. Yet what he did write is crucial. To understand his pride thesis, it is important to understand how he connects pride and sensuality before we move on to feminist and humanistic psychology criticisms. It is to the relationship between pride and addictive desire that we now turn.

3

PRIDE, SENSUALITY
AND ADDICTION

Now the fact that someone desires a temporal good inordinately is due to the fact that he loves himself inordinately.
THOMAS AQUINAS

As we have seen, Niebuhr believes that biblical psychology clearly supports the Augustinian assertion that pride or undue self-love is the dominant factor in human sin. If that is the case, then what is the relationship between this self-centeredness and sensuality, another trait that has also been associated with the concept of sin? Put differently, what is the connection between excessive self-focus and self-indulgence?

Niebuhr is aware that much of Christian thought has focused on sin as the expression of sensuality or excessive desire. He defines *sensuality* as "the self's undue identification with and devotion to particular impulses and desires within itself."[1] He goes on to list various expressions of sensuality: "sexual license, gluttony, extravagance, drunkenness, and abandonment to various forms of physical desire."[2] A more elaborate definition regards these as the fleshly activities that block a concern with divine matters. So Niebuhr raises these difficult questions: Is sensuality simply a form of selfishness? Is

---

[1]Reinhold Niebuhr, *The Nature and Destiny of Man,* vol. 1 (New York: Charles Scribner's, 1964), p. 228.
[2]Ibid.

sensuality a consequence of selfishness? Or instead, is sensuality a distinct form of sin that is not necessarily related to pride?

In spite of a strand of Christian thought that focuses on sin as a love of pleasure, Niebuhr believes that the larger segment of the Christian tradition sees the problems of hedonism as secondary to the problem of pride. The sins of sensuality may be more obvious than the sin of pride, but they are not as deeply rooted. The pillar for this Pauline-Augustinian interpretation of the primacy of pride is the first chapter of Romans, beginning with verse 21 and continuing to the end of the chapter:

> For though they knew God, they did not honor him as God or give thanks to him, but they became futile in their thinking, and their sense-less minds were darkened. Claiming to be wise, they became fools; and they exchanged the glory of the immortal God for images resembling a mortal human being or birds or four-footed animals or reptiles.
>
> Therefore God gave them up in the lusts of their hearts to impurity, to the degrading of their bodies among themselves, because they ex-changed the truth about God for a lie and worshiped and served the creature rather than the Creator, who is blessed forever! Amen.
>
> For this reason God gave them up to degrading passions. . . .
>
> And since they did not see fit to acknowledge God, God gave them up to a debased mind and to things that should not be done. (Rom 1:21-26, 28)

In this passage, it seems clear that the dishonoring of God by placing our-selves as the center of the universe sets us up for disordered desires. Pride and self-deification, the replacement of God with self, throw the rest of our lives out of balance. We lose our center and cannot order our lives properly.

Augustine also argues strongly that sin arises not from the flesh but from idolatry.[3] He offers an interesting explanation: If sin rises from the flesh it-self, then the devil is exonerated from sin because he has no flesh! The first sin is spiritual. Again, the elevation of self precedes our problems with our bodies. Excessive self-indulgence, whatever the form, is a consequence of undue pride.

---

[3] Augustine *City of God* 14.3, trans. Henry Bettenson (New York: Penguin Classics, 1972).

Thomas Aquinas also views excessive desire as an outgrowth of self-love. He thinks the problem of lust, or concupiscence, is a result of humanity's turn from God and worship of self:

> God bestowed his favor upon man in his primitive state, that as long as his mind was subject to God, the lower powers of his soul would be subject to his rational mind, and his body to his soul. But inasmuch as through sin man's mind withdrew from subjection to God, the result was that neither were his lower powers wholly subject to his reason; and from this there followed so great a rebellion of carnal appetite against reason that neither was the body subject to the soul; whence arose death and other bodily defects. . . . Every sinful act proceeds from inordinate desire of a mutable good.[4]

When God is not treated as the source and center of our existence, our desires, which are not bad in themselves, become disoriented and excessive. Torn from our foundation, we anxiously attempt to drown ourselves in the pursuit of every type of passion. When God is negated as the center of our life, human volition becomes disturbed. Off balance, we are given over to a variety of vocations that are never an expression of our created nature. As our pride pushes the divine out of our life, so sensuality binds our will in its sometimes reckless search for expression. Our desires are "disordered" because we have lost our connection to ultimate significance, our relationship with God.

Niebuhr pushes the relationship between pride and sensuality with the following question:

> The question is: does the drunkard or the glutton merely press self-love to the limit and lose all control over himself by his effort to gratify a particular desire so unreservedly that its gratification comes in conflict with other desires? Or is lack of moderation an effort to escape from the self? And does sexual license mean merely the subordination of another person to the ego's self-love, expressed in this case in an inordinate physical desire; or does undisciplined sex life represent an ef-

---

[4]Thomas Aquinas *Summa Theologiae* 2.164.1.

fort on the part of a disquieted and disorganized self to escape from itself? Is sensuality, in other words, a form of idolatry which makes the self god; or is it an alternative idolatry in which the self, conscious of the inadequacy of its self-worship, seeks to escape by finding some other god?[5]

This is an interesting issue. Is sensuality an outpouring of self-love, a way of extending the self in an idolatrous intensification of the self's pleasures? Or is sensuality a retreat from the tensions of being a self, a refusal to face the realities of our existence? The first road to sensuality uses pleasure in the service of the self, a self that feels entitled to unlimited rights. Here, the self clearly becomes a god. The second road to sensuality uses pleasure to avoid the self. Instead of self-worship, it attempts to escape the burdens of being a self by submerging itself in various forms of sensuality. In fact, it turns some finite, limited pleasure into a god. This finite god offers salvation, the means of escaping the turmoils of selfhood. Lacking the courage to be a self, it fixates on any substance, process or person that helps it escape anxiety.

Niebuhr uses the example of luxurious or extravagant living to demonstrate both sides of sensuality.[6] From one view, a rich lifestyle can certainly be seen as the expansive self's attempt to gain status and prestige. Luxury helps fuel the process of self-adoration and can be called an extension of self-love. From a different view, lavish living can be interpreted as a frantic effort to escape from the inner turmoils of selfhood by drowning in the surrounding luxury. Rather than being primarily a form of self-indulgence connected to pride, it is instead an attempt at self-avoidance. Sometimes we throw ourselves into anything that will help us forget the ambiguities of our inner life, or what Niebuhr frequently calls an "uneasy conscience."

Niebuhr also uses drunkenness as an example of both types of sensuality. It has the same ambivalence of purpose. On the one hand, a person can use alcohol to gain a sense of power and importance. The self is thus given center stage. However, drunkenness can also be an attempt not to enhance the ego but to get away from it. Thus, Niebuhr describes "the first purpose of intoxication as the sinful ego-assertion which is rooted in anxiety and un-

---

[5]Niebuhr, *Nature and Destiny of Man*, 1:233.
[6]Ibid., 1:234.

duly compensates for the sense of inferiority and insecurity; while the second purpose of intoxication springs from the sense of guilt, or a state of perplexity in which a sense of guilt has been compounded with the previous sense of insecurity."[7] As such, the self-avoidance it also entails depicts "the logic of sin which every heart reveals: Anxiety tempts the self to sin; the sin increases the insecurity which it was intended to alleviate until some escape from the whole tension of life is sought."[8]

Sex is another example of both self-indulgent and self-avoidant sensuality. Clearly, promiscuity can be easily recognized as the servant of self-deification. New experiences and sexual "conquests" contribute to this self-adulation. Worshiping the advancement of self, others are mere objects to manipulate. On the other hand, sexual passion can be a detour from the self and a way of deifying one's partner. Instead of making a god out of self, one substitutes the partner as the divine. The godlike partner becomes the focus of our ultimate concern. Pointing toward both self-deification and other-deification in sex, Niebuhr makes an extremely interesting observation which predates many current discussions on the nature of sexual and romantic "addiction":

> This is what gives man's sex life the quality of uneasiness. It is both a vehicle of the primal sin of self-deification and the expression of an uneasy conscience, seeking to escape from self by the deification of the other. The deification of the other is almost a literal description of many romantic sentiments in which attributes of perfection are assigned to the partner of love, beyond the capacities of any human being to bear, and therefore the cause of inevitable disillusionment. While the more active part of the male and the more passive part of the female in the relation of the sexes may seem to point toward self-deification as the particular sin of the male and the idolatry of the other as the particular temptation of the woman in the sexual act, yet both elements of sin are undoubtedly involved in both sexes.[9]

Both forms of sensuality involve idolatry. In one, self-glorification substi-

---

[7]Ibid., 1:234–35.
[8]Ibid., 1:235.
[9]Ibid., 1:237.

tutes for God. In the other, another person is worshiped as the ground and source of one's existence.

Niebuhr also acknowledges a third way that sexual passion can be used as a vehicle of sensuality. Sexuality itself, not the adoration of our sexual partner, can be worshiped as another escape from self. Even if self-worship has been frustrated and worship of another has been disenchanted, sexual activity, like intoxication, can be used as a tool of self-avoidance. Instead of a flight toward another god, Niebuhr calls this a flight toward nothingness. Its primary concern is to escape the painful daylight of human consciousness.

> Whether in drunkenness, gluttony, sexual license, love of luxury, or any inordinate devotion to a mutable good, sensuality is always: (1) an extension of self-love to the point where it defeats its own ends; (2) an effort to escape the prison house of self by finding a god in a process or person outside the self; and (3) finally an effort to escape from the confusion which sin has created into some form of subconscious existence.[10]

Regardless of which form of sensuality we pursue, it is built on the failure to trust God as the center of our world. Thus, we rely on our own resources to solve our anxiety problem. In trusting our own resolutions, rather than God, we become preoccupied with eliminating our anxieties. The attempts to eliminate our condition make the condition worse. For Niebuhr, *any solution to the problem of human existence that does not trust in God is an expression of pride.* Why? Because we are placing at the helm of our lives our own solutions instead of relying on divine assurance. This may not look like an obvious form of puffed-up self-congratulatory pride. But pride is inherent in *any* form of God-replacement. Distrust in God and human pride are always two parts of a single process. This point will be important to remember when we later look at feminist critiques of the Augustinian tradition.

It is crucial to remember that sensuality is not simply our natural impulses. It is not "animal instincts" because animal life is innocent of unlimited and demonic potencies. Instead, it is an attempt, however

---

[10]Ibid., 1:239-40.

misguided, to solve the problem of insecurity by replacing God as the Source of our existence.

Sensuality can involve excessive attachments to any number of unfulfilling enslavements, which have sometimes been called addictions.[11] Addictions always have the character of placing infinite investment in finite things. Idolatry is inevitable for both substance addictions (alcohol, cocaine, heroin) and process addictions (gambling, work, sex or any compulsive behavior). Put simply, *something* becomes *everything*. The end result, of course, is what Gerald May calls a kidnapping of our attention.[12] A brief exploration of the dynamics of addiction can help clarify Niebuhr's views on sensuality and its relationship to pride.

SENSUALITY, CONCUPISCENCE AND ADDICTION: FROM AUGUSTINE TO GERALD MAY

Augustine's discussion of sensuality is centered around the word *concupiscence*.[13] In fact, no writer in Western history has emphasized the significance of concupiscence as much as Augustine. The word comes from the Latin *concupiscere,* which means to strive after, to covet or to long for and desire. The New Testament word is *epithymia* (Col 3:5; 1 Thess 4:5), which refers to sensual desire associated with envy, greed, avarice and coveting. Yet concupiscence does not simply mean ordinary desire. Instead, it refers to inordinate desire, an insatiable lust. By concupiscence, Augustine generally refers to the Pauline lusts of the flesh versus the spirit (Rom 7; Gal 5:17). This disorderly desire results from our disconnection from God as the center of our lives. It is a wide reservoir out of which particular obsessions and compulsive attachments emerge. It prompts a preoccupation with this world's goods.

Concupiscence, therefore, refers to the spiritual condition behind compulsive attachments. As desire-out-of-control, it invariably leads to idolatry, the making of a limited, finite good into a god. But again, it seeks this god

---

[11]For an excellent elaboration of addiction as inordinate desire, see Gerald May, *Addiction and Grace* (San Francisco: Harper & Row, 1988).

[12]Ibid.

[13]Augustine *City of God* 14; *Confessions,* trans. Henry Chadwick (New York: Oxford University Press, 1991).

because a relationship with the divine has already been abandoned. In spite of the fact that lust's target provides only temporary relief, concupiscent craving continues to seek more and more. It panics at the thought of its desired object being taken away. For Augustine, as well as Niebuhr, concupiscence always involves the love of created things apart from their Creator. John Hugo offers a very helpful definition of Augustinian concupiscence:

> Concupiscence, therefore, in Augustine's thought, is the disorderly pursuit by the several appetites of their proper natural goods, a pursuit which, since the loss of integrity, is difficult even for the grace-filled will to contain within the prescribed limits. This concupiscence, tending toward exuberance and turbulence (one of Augustine's favorite words) leads readily to disorder, diverting from the will of God. Concupiscence is not, therefore, as the Pelagians maintained, a merely natural vigor by which the faculties appropriately seek their own goods: it is a powerful vital energy that spontaneously rises to excess, tempting the will from God.[14]

Having moved away from a trust in God, we involve ourselves in habitual, destructive enjoyments of inferior goods as replacements for God. Again, concupiscence and idolatry are two sides of the same coin. In fact, we can speak of concupiscence as an inherent proclivity toward idolatry. We human beings have a nasty habit of trying to turn something finite into the infinite. To repeat: for Augustine concupiscence is not the most basic dilemma. Concupiscence is instead a secondary problem following quickly behind the prideful replacement of God. Our desires are disordered *because* we have lost our center in God.

Margaret Miles suggests that we must understand the existential anxiety about "missing out" in order to grasp the significance of Augustinian concupiscence. As she puts it, "Augustine's astoundingly accurate description of *concupiscentia* as a repetition compulsion, a frantic pursuit of frustratingly elusive pleasure, does reveal the totalitarian scope of his anxiety."[15] We constantly grab at objects in a frenzied fear that something will be lost to us. Miles re-

---

[14]John Hugo, *St. Augustine on Nature, Sex, and Marriage* (Chicago: Scepter, 1969), p. 55.
[15]Margaret Miles, *Desire and Delight: A New Reading of Augustine's Confessions* (New York: Crossroad, 1992).

minds us that Augustine's attitude toward concupiscence was actually one of sympathy more than judgment. He knew all too well that compulsive pursuits end up in much pain and suffering, and are therefore to be pitied.[16]

It is very easy to assume that the notion of concupiscence points only toward sexual lust. There is no question that Augustine, out of his own struggles with libido, may have exaggerated this claim. I take Augustine's description of his own sexual compulsivity at face value and assume it was indeed a very difficult battle for him. Yet it seems likely that Augustine uses his own sexual obsession as an example of obsession in general. Sexual lust becomes a model for understanding the nature and dynamics of concupiscence.

As Miles points out, after identifying the basic structure of concupiscence as pleasureless desire, Augustine does not tell us a lot of juicy, carnal stories, which we might expect.[17] He frustrates our voyeuristic curiosity by pointing toward stealing from a pear tree as an example of the character of concupiscence. This illustrates, I believe, that it is not sexual lust per se that is the enemy, but compulsive lust in general. Stephen Duffy agrees: "It is wrongheaded, however, to read him [Augustine] as wholly identifying original sin or concupiscence with sexual desire. The disorder of sexual desire is a symptom produced by Adam's and our own disordered wills. Unable to love the supreme Good above all, *all* our loves and desires are disordered."[18] Perhaps if he were living in our own day, Augustine might use compulsive consumerism as a primary example of concupiscence. James Kavanaugh certainly makes a good case for this point.[19]

Patrick McCormick believes that contemporary studies of addiction offer a new paradigm for understanding sin as concupiscence.[20] McCormick accepts the definition of *addiction* as a "pathological relationship to a mood-altering experience which has life damaging consequences."[21] He goes on to say that "within the pathological relationship the addict believes he has

---

[16]Ibid., chap. 1.

[17]Ibid.

[18]Stephen J. Duffy, *The Dynamics of Grace: Perspectives in Theological Anthropology* (Collegeville, Minn.: Michael Glazier, 1993), p. 92.

[19]John F. Kavanaugh, *Following Christ in a Consumer Society* (New York: Orbis, 1981).

[20]Patrick McCormick, *Sin as Addiction* (Mahwah, N.J.: Paulist, 1989).

[21]This is probably the most widely used definition of *addiction* in contemporary addiction/recovery literature. It was formulated and used throughout Patrick Carnes's work. See, especially, *Out of the Shadows* (Minneapolis, Minn.: CompCare, 1988).

found a constant, repeatable, and ultimately dependable substance which is capable of relieving the pain of life by introducing a 'happiness' solution."[22] In his understanding of addiction, McCormick follows the lead of many addiction specialists by including both substance (alcohol, cocaine) and process addictions (gambling, sex, spending, etc.). While offering momentary relief, it is the character of all addiction to develop an obsessive, life-damaging attachment to a limited earthly good. The problem is usually not the activity itself. Instead, it is the bondage to that activity. The addict's will becomes enslaved to the experience. Freedom is diminished as the will becomes bound: "Addictions begin by seeming to offer a solution to a person's pain. Later they become part of that pain, and finally they become the most deadly problem confronting the person."[23] Refusing to accept their own limitations and creatureliness, addicts inevitably commit idolatry in that the mood-altering experience becomes a god.

McCormick points out some of the ways in which sin and addiction parallel each other:

> It would seem therefore that structurally sin operates as an addiction in a number of ways. The sinner is like an addict—denying his/her creatureliness, refusing to let God be God, creating a delusional world through deception, denial and projection, becoming alienated from all others and destroying the self in a spiral of disintegration ending in death.[24]

Similarly, salvation and recovery go hand in hand. Listen to his poignant description of twelve-step recovery programs:

> Finally, the therapeutic approach to the "twelve steps" is profoundly (if not specifically) Christian. It invites persons and communities to surrender idolatrous fixations, accept the goodness of creation and their place in it, and make an ongoing act of faith in the loving fidelity of God and the creative splendor of life. It calls us to enter into open and trusting relationships with our God, our neighbor, creation and

---

[22]McCormick, *Sin as Addiction*, p. 149.
[23]Ibid., p. 154.
[24]Ibid., p. 163.

ourselves, to accept our creatureliness in gratitude and hope, and to reach out in love to others in pain.[25]

In short, McCormick is convinced that addiction provides a vivid portrait of the dynamics of sin. The problem of addictiveness (concupiscence) is far greater than particular addictions (what Augustine calls "actual sins"). The utter helplessness and hopelessness in the vulnerable world of addiction is an important prelude to encountering God's grace.

Also like Augustine, Gerald May, a contemplative psychiatrist and addiction specialist, believes that our deepest longing is an inborn desire for God—a term he uses without specific Judeo-Christian content.[26] We may experience this in many ways, such as a longing for wholeness, completion or fulfillment. Regardless of how we describe it, it is primarily a longing for love. We have, May believes, a hunger to love, to be loved and to move closer to the ultimate Source of love. He tells us that "this yearning is the essence of the human spirit."[27]

So what's the problem? May believes that we continually give ourselves over to things we do not really want or things that we find unsatisfying. The reason for this is tied to the problem of addiction. May defines *addiction* as "a state of compulsion, obsession, or preoccupation that enslaves a person's will and desire."[28] Addiction attaches desire. The word *attachment* is crucial to May's notion of addiction. Addiction attaches desire by bonding and enslaving the energy of desire to certain specific behaviors, things and people. The objects of attachment then become obsessions and preoccupations. The entrapment is so severe that our attempts to break free only push us deeper into it. Or, as May puts it, "it is the very nature of addiction to *feed* on our attempts to master it."[29]

May very accurately points out that traditional psychotherapy has failed miserably in the treatment of addiction. Countless well-meaning individuals have made heroic Pelagian attempts to eliminate their addiction through an act of the will. For many, the result has been despair, self-disgust and a

---

[25]Ibid., p. 174.
[26]May, *Addiction and Grace.*
[27]Ibid., p. 1.
[28]Ibid., p. 14.
[29]Ibid., p. 4 (italics in original).

deeper spiraling into the grip of addiction. Addiction, says May, is "the most powerful psychic enemy of humanity's desire for God."[30]

While speaking as a psychiatrist, May also resurrects the old religious word *idolatry* as having extreme relevance for understanding the dynamics of addiction. The object of our addiction is what we worship, what we attend to, where we give our time and energy. We never really love our attachment, because love presupposes a certain degree of freedom. The intensity of the enslavement may *feel* like love, but again, we cannot love that which takes away our freedom. Addiction "kidnaps" our attention, and we are left hostages to tyrannical desires.

Like Augustine, May believes that the only thing in the universe more powerful than addiction is the experience of grace. Once again, May's conviction does not come from a theological education or religious work. Instead, this conviction arose from his "secular" experience of working with addicted people.

Also like Augustine, May argues for the universality of inordinate desire. It's everyone's dilemma. It is quite easy for us to point toward the alcoholic lying in the gutter or the cocaine addict snorting away this month's paycheck and say, "Now *that's* an addict." However, for May, "it is as if these severely addicted people have played out, on an extreme scale, a drama that all human beings experience more subtly and more covertly."[31]

Perhaps the least obvious, but not least powerful, form of bonding attachments are the security addictions. Possessions, power and human relationships represent false gods to which we are frequently enslaved. Possessive addictions have to do with income and property. Power addictions include status, influence, and control. Human relationship addictions involve dependency or possessiveness. Much like Augustine, who talked about a tendency to devour people, rather than "love them in God," May believes the intensity of desire for someone is often confused with love. All forms of addiction, of course, attempt to take away the anxiety involved in being human. Again, we see the Kierkegaardian-Niebuhrian theme of anxiety operating as the *precondition* of sin or addictiveness.

---

[30]Ibid., p. 3.
[31]Ibid., p. 43.

Particular addictions, then, or what Augustine calls actual sins, stem from a much larger problem of compulsivity and addictiveness. The human condition of addictiveness, reminiscent of original sin, is inevitable and inescapable. Pelagian efforts at preventive mental health education may be helpful, but we're probably not going to change the central theme of human nature: we are idolaters who invariably get our priorities mixed up, attend to inferior things, turn away from love, and get attached to something that we hope will rid us of our anxieties.

Gerald May has provided an excellent analysis of the precondition of addiction. He offers, in my view, a very insightful, contemporary retelling of the Augustinian story of sin. Humanity's inevitable, but not necessary, turning away from divine love sets up an imbalance within each of us. We are off center and, as a consequence, attach ourselves to finite goods, which leave us restless and insatiable. We develop a tolerance for these temporary fixes and avoid the source of our dilemma—distrust in our Creator. While some have expressed concern that the idea of sin could be absorbed into the concept of addiction, the way May describes the spiritual backdrop of addiction's dilemma is most informative for a relevant doctrine of sin.[32]

BACK TO THE PRIDE VERSUS SELF-CONTEMPT CONFLICT

It is widely known that Niebuhr has made a lasting contribution to twelve-step programs through his famous "Serenity Prayer." This prayer is repeated at the beginning of every twelve-step meeting. Niebuhr's emphasis on the issue of human pride and egocentricity has also become very important for these groups. The placing of our own ego where we should be acknowledging a "higher power" (God) is a consistent theme in Alcoholics Anonymous. So persistent is this idea that an acronym for ego (E.G.O.) has become "easing God out." The somewhat humorous comment frequently made to newcomers in A.A. meetings declares: "All you need to know about God for now is that 'you ain't him.'" Indeed, Ernest Kurtz, in his exploration of Alcoholics Anonymous, titled his book *Not-God* largely because every alcoholic has to learn that he or she is not the center of the

---

[32]See Linda Mercandante, *Sinners and Victims* (Louisville, Ky.: Westminster John Knox, 1996).

universe. Kurtz offers a fascinating interpretation of the Creation story as a tale about alcoholism:

> In the Garden of Eden, Adam and Eve had sinned by reaching for more than had been given. They ate of the forbidden fruit because the serpent promised that eating it would make them "as Gods." Their punishment was the loss of the garden they had once been given. The alcoholic, in drinking, had sought inappropriate control over reality— more than was granted to human finitude. The promise of alcohol was likewise one of Godlike control: alcoholic drinking sought to control how outside reality impinged upon the alcoholic as well as his own moods, feelings, and emotions. As in the mythic parallel, the penalty for such abuse was the loss of any ability to use properly: reaching for more than had been given resulted in the loss of even that which had been given. To this understanding, the alcoholic surrendered by the very admission: "I am an alcoholic."[33]

Bill Wilson, the cofounder of Alcoholics Anonymous, frequently described alcoholism as "self-will run riot."[34] By his own confession, this matched his experience of drinking as an extension of pride and self-exaltation. Alcohol was part of his grandiosity and desire to be center-stage.

Thus, the Augustinian-Niebuhrian emphasis on God-replacement (hence, pride) as the crucial factor in addiction prompts many twelve-step groups to identify a strong spiritual component in addiction. Disconnected from a balancing Source (God), we attach ourselves to limited, finite things. This process involves both distrust and pride. Distrusting a reliance on God, we seek an "easier, softer way" that attempts to detour our finitude and places self at the center of our lives. Having pridefully replaced God with the self and its own anxiety-reducing strategies, we actually increase our anxiety and, hence, drive ourselves more deeply into our compulsive attachments. Thus, the experience of addiction frequently revives the Augustinian-Niebuhrian emphasis on the way God is "eased out" of our

---

[33]Ernest Kurtz, *Not-God: A History of Alcoholics Anonymous* (Center City, Minn.: Hazelden Educational Services, 1979), p. 182.

[34]Bill W[ilson], *Alcoholics Anonymous: The Story of How More Than One Hundred Men Have Recovered from Alcoholism* (New York: A.A. World Services/Works Publishing, 1939).

lives, the self takes over and compulsivity reigns. Surely this offers another testimony to the destructive power of human pride.

BUT IS PRIDE THE PROBLEM FOR EVERYONE?

While the connection between addiction and self-exaltation can readily be seen in many, is this a dominantly male experience? Is pride always the culprit behind a destructive lifestyle, or is it possible that low self-esteem or even self-contempt could be the major factor? Can some gravitate toward compulsive attachments or addictions because they have miserable self-images and are "down on themselves"? Does further warning about a pride problem simply push some individuals, particularly women, deeper into self-abandonment, self-avoidance and low self-esteem? Asked directly, is pride really primary in all sin? Having pointed toward the strength of the Augustinian-Niebuhrian pride thesis, it is now time to examine its possible limitations. We will explore two sources of criticism: (a) a group of important feminist theologians who believe the pride paradigm does not describe most women's experience and (b) the humanistic psychotherapy assertion, found most notably in Rogers, that pride is rarely *anyone's* major problem. It is to the feminist critiques of the pride thesis that we now turn.

4

PRIDE AND SELF-LOSS

Theology, insofar as it focuses on the sin of pride, not only neglects women's experience, but adds to the pressures that keep women from being "women and persons" by suggesting that self-assertion and the struggle for self-definition are sins.
JUDITH PLASKOW

An exhausted woman attends a Sunday church service looking for some comfort and strength to face the upcoming week. Her life seems so concerned with the needs of her children, the expectations of her husband, the demands of her employer and the domestic tasks surrounding her that she is worn out. Somehow, she, as a person, seems to be drowning in her relationships. She needs more help from her husband, she knows she needs to quit enabling her kids, and she recognizes that she needs to break her approval-seeking patterns at work.

Within this woman is a small, but growing voice of assertiveness and justice. Perhaps it is time to be her own ally and stand up for herself. She has denied her own thoughts, feelings and preferences for so long that she will have to work hard to rediscover what they are. She awaits the sermon as she hopes to find a source that will nourish *her* spirit, *her* identity, *her* courage.

The topic of the sermon is sin. She listens as the minister begins a vehement denouncement of arrogance, self-centeredness, selfishness and self-exaltation. A blistering attack on the human ego accompanies a severe warning about the dangers of pride. She listens, straining to see how this energetic description of sin applies to her. She hears much talk about an in-flated, rather than deflated, will.

Then the minister switches gears and begins talking about the antidote to this horrendous problem of pride. What we need, says the minister, is greater self-sacrifice. Our "me generation," or narcissistic culture, needs to reclaim the meaning of selfless service to others. If pride is the sin, then humility is the cure. And for this minister, humility has to do with the shrinking, rather than the expanding, self. It is clearly assumed that everyone in the congregation struggles with an overvalued self. The fact that some members may have an underdeveloped self is never even considered.

This woman, who has been struggling with the courage to become more self-assertive and recognize that she has some rights, is invited to throw these discoveries overboard and sink back into a selfless world of passivity. Pride is the enemy, so God forbid that she should think of herself first! Her lifestyle of selflessness, her fear of her own freedom and her self-destructive accommodations to others are all given a religious endorsement. Implicitly, she is praised for maintaining the status quo, avoiding her inner life and losing herself in her relationships.

Three things may have happened during the sermon. First, the sermon's denunciation of pride and self-centeredness most likely leaves her feeling guilty for her tentative longings to assert herself and care for herself. On the other hand, a second possibility is that because sin has been defined strictly as excessive self-concern or pride, she may feel innocent and sinless. After all, this kind of self-aggrandizement is not her problem. In fact, it may be quite easy for her to feel an unconscious sense of self-righteousness because she is not a selfish person. Second, her possibility of becoming assertive has been greatly derailed by a sermon focusing on the wretchedness of self-interest. Her motivation to stand up for herself has been discouraged. After all, she doesn't want to end up being another self-centered person in a highly narcissistic culture.

It does not dawn on her that she may not be as "innocent" as she appears. While she may not exhibit the type of sin being described, perhaps she's involved in another sin, the sin of participating in her own exploitation. Perhaps the refusal to pay attention to her own inner voice is a sinful shrinking away from her God-given potential. Perhaps the inner world of freedom, decision making and self-direction would be much too frightening to face. Maybe she is accepting, and therefore reinforcing, the very patterns that are making her miserable.

She has been listening to a clergyman who is probably battling with his own pride problem. In fact, this male minister may be projecting his pride demon onto his entire congregation. Perhaps the men in the crowd are nodding their heads in agreement, yet some of the women have great difficulty relating to what is being said. Even more, self-sacrifice, touted as the primary ingredient for change, may push these women deeper into an underworld of miserable selflessness.

Is self-inflation truly the problem for *everyone?* Feminist theologians such as Valerie Saiving, Daphne Hampson, Susan Nelson Dunfee, Judith Plaskow and Serene Jones question the Augustinian-Niebuhrian thesis that pride is the root of all sin.[1] For them, sin does not always emerge from an overvalued self. They believe the pride thesis is far more descriptive of men than women. In fact, they think that women struggle more with the failure to *be* a self than with self-aggrandizement. As early as 1960, Saiving described very well this problem of a male-dominated view of sin in Christian thought:

> For the temptations of woman *as woman* are not the same as the temptations of man *as man,* and the specifically feminine forms of sin— "feminine" not because they are confined to women or because women are incapable of sinning in other ways but because they are outgrowths of the basic feminine character structure—have a quality which can never be encompassed by such terms as "pride" and "will-to-power." They are better suggested by such items as triviality, distractibility, and diffuseness; lack of an organizing center or focus; dependence on others for one's own self-definition; tolerance at the expense of standards of excellence; inability to respect the boundaries

---

[1] Valerie Saiving, "The Human Situation: A Feminine View," in *Womanspirit Rising: A Feminist Reader in Religion,* ed. Carol P. Christ and Judith Plaskow (San Francisco: Harper & Row, 1979); Daphne Hampson, "Reinhold Niebuhr on Sin: A Critique," in *Reinhold Niebuhr and the Issues of Our Time,* ed. R. Harries (Grand Rapids, Mich.: Eerdmans, 1986); Susan Nelson Dunfee, "The Sin of Hiding: A Feminist Critique of Reinhold Niebuhr's Account of the Sin of Pride," *Soundings* 65, no. 3 (1982): 316-26; Judith Plaskow, *Sex, Sin, and Grace: Women's Experience and the Theologies of Reinhold Niebuhr and Paul Tillich* (Lanham, Md.: University Press of America, 1980).

of privacy; sentimentality, gossipy sociability, and mistrust of reason—
in short, underdevelopment or negation of the self.[2]

Note here that Saiving is not reading human history in a manner that suggests that men are sinners and women are completely innocent. She is saying that men and women sin differently.

For Saiving, the Augustinian tradition's emphasis on pride leads to the
belief that the solution for everyone, male and female, is self-sacrificial love.
In other words, pride and self-sacrificial love are dependent concepts. Self-
sacrifice is redemptive precisely because an undue self-focus has already
occurred. Once you diagnose the human condition as excessively self-
focused, the obvious cure will be a selfless service to others.

Expanding on Saiving's work, Plaskow has written what is probably the
most comprehensive feminist critique of Niebuhr.[3] For Plaskow, women's
experience has not involved self-assertion and pride so much as self-abnegation and the underdevelopment of self. In fact, Plaskow challenges the
whole history of Christian thought insofar as it has focused primarily on
men's experience of sin. After all, isolated men have been the primary con-
structors of theology. The result has been the ignoring of women's experience. Further, the emphasis on the redeeming character of self-sacrificial
love (so needed for prideful men) can actually push women even deeper
into their own type of sin as it reinforces self-loss.

This is not to say that Plaskow does not appreciate Niebuhr's insights on
the male propensity for self-elevation. Nor does she say that this description
never applies to women. However, Niebuhr claims to be describing *human*
experience, and for her, he is not describing the dominant experience of
women. Put simply, Niebuhr is talking to other men. Plaskow's problems
with Niebuhrian sin are focused on the following issues: (a) sensuality
should not be seen as merely a byproduct of pride, but as a problem in its
own right, (b) Niebuhr employs more than one definition of *sensuality,* and
(c) he lays out a mistaken sequence of the development of sensuality.

Plaskow believes Niebuhr is wrong in subordinating sensuality under
pride. In fact, she wonders why Niebuhr has ordered sin in this way. While

---

[2]Saiving, "The Human Situation," p. 37.
[3]Plaskow, *Sex, Sin, and Grace.*

this has been the dominant model of the tradition, she points out that in other matters, such as original sin, Niebuhr feels most comfortable in revising tradition.[4] She believes the evidence does not support the claimed secondary nature of sensuality. However, it is not simply a matter of Niebuhr's subordinating sensuality under pride. Her problem is that Niebuhr does not recognize sensuality as a significant, independent form of sin. Niebuhr fails to deal with those aspects of sensuality that do not seem to flow from pride. Plaskow recognizes that sinful self-negation may sometimes be linked to the female pride of power. However, Niebuhr is mistaken about the scope of male pride as the primary source for sin:

> Niebuhr's doctrine of humanity can certainly accommodate the insight that human beings may attempt to escape the contradictions of their nature by denying the unlimited possibilities of human freedom. Niebuhr's view of human nature, however, does not ground an equally complex doctrine of sin. In dealing with sin, he seems to forget the burdensome world of freedom and to concentrate on the exaltation of it. . . . Human beings can ignore their finitude but they can also fail to live up to obligations of their freedom. The refusal of self-transcendence ought to be, if one uses Niebuhr's categories, no less a sin than pride—a sin against oneself, against other persons, and against God. If pride is the attempt to usurp the place of God, sensuality is the denial of creation in his image.[5]

Plaskow points toward a couple of reasons that women may refuse the path of self-assertion and sink back into a "selfless" existence.[6] One traditional reason has been material. Being selfless has sometimes had the financial reward of being economically supported. The second reason is that selflessness has also helped women avoid the burdensome world of freedom and difficult decisions. Plaskow says of this selfless condition, "Insofar as women accept this status for its rewards and welcome relief from the burden of freedom, they are guilty of complicity in their own oppression; they sin."[7]

---

[4]Ibid., p. 62.
[5]Ibid., pp. 66-68.
[6]Ibid., p. 64.
[7]Ibid., pp. 64-65.

This retreat from self involves the sin of "missing the mark" of our authentic humanity. Sin is therefore rejecting the journey, denying the freedom, resting comfortably in a "borrowed" existence. The "shrinking self" is as dangerous as the exalted self. Sin is saying, "I am nobody worth becoming." It is an unwillingness to assert what Paul Tillich calls the "courage to be."[8]

Plaskow opposes what she perceives as a sequence involved with the problem of sensuality. She uses Niebuhr's discussion of sexuality as an example. She recalls Niebuhr's comment that sinful sexuality moves from (1) a desire to dominate the other in an attempt at self-assertion, to (2) an idolatrous worship of the other as the center of one's existence and (3) an effort to drown oneself in the subconscious world of the senses. Whether or not Niebuhr intends this pattern as a developmental sequence seems unclear to me, but Plaskow reads Niebuhr this way. In other words, she believes Niebuhr is saying that unhealthy sexuality is first an attempt to dominate. When that is frustrated, we move into a worship of the other. After disenchantment with the other, we look toward sex itself as an escape-from-self mechanism. Plaskow acknowledges that each one of these motivations may be the dominant factor, but she insists that one does not necessarily follow from the other. She believes that a failure at self-assertion does not always precede a flight from self. Sometimes the attempt at self-assertion, especially for women socially prohibited from that experience, has never been made in the first place.

Daphne Hampson presents another reason that Niebuhr and the Augustinian tradition are one-sided in their analysis of sin. While Niebuhr is very indebted to Kierkegaard, he does not follow his mentor in distinguishing between "manly" and "womanly" forms of sin. By interpreting male selfishness as the primary *human* experience of hubris, Niebuhr ignores the womanly sin of failing to be a self. As Hampson reminds us, Kierkegaard distinguishes male egotism (trying to be yourself by yourself) from the sin of not being willing to be yourself. A frequent way in which women have not been themselves is through losing themselves in another. Hampson writes: "I am not faulting Niebuhr's analysis. It is surely illuminating. I am simply saying that it is a description of what is peculiarly male temptation."[9]

---

[8]Paul Tillich, *The Courage to Be* (New Haven, Conn.: Yale University Press, 1952).
[9]Hampson, "Reinhold Niebuhr on Sin," p. 47.

The male, with his inflated ego, is not content with his actual (creaturely) self. Instead, he lusts to rise above himself. He desires to expand beyond the limited confines of the actual self into the idealized self.[10]

A woman, on the other hand, often refuses to be herself and instead loses herself in another. The anxiety of being a self is abandoned as she invests all her energy in others. Hardly a self-sufficient, isolated individual, she has abnegated responsibility for herself. The last thing in the world she needs to hear is that she should stop exploiting others and start sacrificing for them. Her task is to *become a self,* not give up a self she has never found in the first place. As Hampson puts it, "To tell such a woman that it is the sin of pride to seek self-fulfillment is to reinforce her form of sin: her dispersal of herself in others, her unwanted serving of them, her attempt to live through them, and her self-disparagement."[11]

Hampson reminds us that the primary task for men is to find themselves *in relationship,* while the primary task for women is to find *themselves* in relationship.[12] Following Kierkegaard, she recognizes that either sex may have "manly" or "womanly" types of sin. However, her point remains that men dominantly manifest the overvalued self while women fall prey to an undervalued self, and hence, often fail to be a self.

Perhaps the most hazardous thing about the male-intoxicated image of sin is that our image of God, also, is deeply affected:

> The God of the tradition, as we have seen, fits the male system. Indeed he seems to have been modeled on the worst image of the human male. He is isolated, powerful, and the top of the hierarchy. He is said to have aseity: to be entire unto himself! Moreover his supremacy qualifies others. It is by comparison with his goodness that men are to know themselves sinners.[13]

Hampson further adds a Freudian slant on this image of God, saying that it contains the classic, absolute taboo that the son should challenge the fa-

---

[10]I borrow the term "idealized self" from the work of Karen Horney. See, for instance, *Neurosis and Human Growth* (New York: W. W. Norton, 1950).

[11]Ibid., p. 49.

[12]Ibid., p. 55.

[13]Ibid., p. 56.

ther. If Freud is right that sons both revere and are afraid to challenge the authority of their fathers, does this not play into the idea that pride or self-assertion is the primary sin? Men dare not assert themselves against the cosmic Father. Hampson concludes her article with this interesting comment:

> While writing this essay I mentioned to a friend of mine, telling her nothing of the essay's content, that in the tradition the devil was said to be an angel who fell because he tried to fly higher than God. Her spontaneous response: "What sort of a God is that that 'He' should mind that an angel should try to fly higher than 'Him'?!" A different evaluation of society, of the individual and of human relations cannot but significantly affect our understanding of God.[14]

Susan Nelson Dunfee has also criticized Niebuhr for a male-dominated view of sin and suggested that the sin of "hiding" is a better way of describing women's experience.[15] By "hiding" she means the attempt to escape freedom and selfhood. By subsuming the sin of hiding under pride, Niebuhr fails to adequately develop a doctrine of sin that speaks to women's experience. And to make matters worse, his "cure" for sin—namely, self-sacrificial love—pushes women even deeper into hiding. Again, his emphasis on self-sacrificial love as the highest virtue encourages women to persist in a selfless existence:

> Most obviously, by making self-sacrificial love the ultimate Christian virtue, one makes the sin of hiding into a virtue as well, and thereby encouraging those already committing the sin of hiding to stay in that state. One then becomes glorified for never truly seeking to become fully human. Furthermore, by uplifting hiding to a virtue, and by denying the sin of hiding as a possibility Niebuhr's theology has no understanding of how the one guilty of the sin of hiding can be judged in his/her sin and called to actualize his/her freedom. There is no judgment upon the one who escapes; there is no call to emerge from the state of hiddenness.[16]

---

[14]Ibid., p. 58.
[15]Dunfee, "The Sin of Hiding."
[16]Ibid., p. 321.

If pride remains *the* primary sin, the sin of hiding goes unnamed. Oppressed persons remain oppressed because of their own fears of self-assertion.

Instead of a universal focus on the sin of male pride, Rosemary Radford Ruether believes that women may need to consider a different kind of pride, a self-respect that moves them away from the so-called virtues of humility and self-abnegation.[17]

> For Christian women, particularly in more conservative traditions, one of the most difficult barriers to feminist consciousness is the identification of sin with anger and pride, and virtue with humility and self-abnegation. Although this doctrine of sin and virtue supposedly is for "all Christians," it becomes, for women, an ideology that reinforces male-female subjugation and lack of self-esteem. Women become "Christ-like" by having no self of their own. They become the "suffering servants," by accepting male abuse and exploitation. Women are made to feel profoundly guilty and diffident about even the smallest sense of self-affirmation. They fear the beginning steps of asking who they are and what they want to do, rather than "putting others first."[18]

For Ruether, this whole Augustinian paradigm of pride and humility needs to be reevaluated by women. Perhaps women have been too prone to avoid the ambiguities of freedom by making humility their primary virtue. This false sense of humility has diminished the real possibility of self-esteem and appropriate self-regard.

But does this mean that women are not subject to the corrupting power of egoism and pride? Is pride only a male problem? Ruether argues that women, too, are quite capable of falling into arrogance and egoism. Again, self-exaltation is not an inherently gendered form of sin. Instead the problem has resulted more from social and historical factors. "The systems of domination, then, are 'male' only in the historical and sociological sense that males have shaped and benefitted from them, not in the sense that they correspond to unique, evil capacities of males that women do not share.

---

[17]Rosemary Radford Ruether, *Sexism and God-Talk: Toward a Feminist Theology* (Boston: Beacon, 1983), p. 186.

[18]Ibid., pp. 185–86.

Women have no guarantees, because of a different 'nature,' that they will act differently."[19] Thus, while patriarchy has created enormous injustices, it does not therefore follow that men are essentially evil.

PRIDE AND SELF-LOSS:
SOCIALIZED TO SIN DIFFERENTLY?

In arguing that women tend to struggle more with an undervalued self than an overvalued self, feminist theologians are not necessarily saying that women, by their very nature, are less proud than men. If they argued that way, it would place them more on the side of essentialism, rather than constructivism, in feminist theory. Essentialism refers to the position that men and women come into this world prepackaged with male and female characteristics. In other words, gender traits are largely biologically given. While most feminist theorists obviously recognize sex as biologically given, gender, on the other hand, is largely socially constructed. Thus, gender is not pre-social. Few feminist theologians would argue that women inherently, or innately, suffer more from low self-esteem than men. This would be saying that men and women are "hard-wired" to sin differently. Instead, most feminist theologians argue that men and women are socialized to sin differently. Historical and cultural pressures push men and women to deal with their anxiety in different ways.

But can we really speak generically about "men's" and "women's" experience? That issue is sometimes energetically debated in feminist theory and theology. Some argue that other factors such as class and race make individuals of the same gender quite different. Does an upper-middle-class woman teaching feminist theory at a prestigious university really share the same female experience of oppression with an uneducated, economically deprived single mother of five?

Serene Jones, in her insightful work *Feminist Theory and Christian Theology: Cartographies of Grace,* believes that we *can* speak of a general exploitation of women.[20] She quickly adds, however, that finding this commonality can be difficult because individual lives can be so different that they seem to

---

[19]Ibid., p. 188.
[20]Serene Jones, *Feminist Theory and Christian Theology: Cartographies of Grace* (Minneapolis: Fortress, 2000).

resist classification. She believes that all women share in a general experience of oppression, which refers to "dynamic forces, both personal and social, that diminish or deny the flourishing of women."[21] She believes this definition of oppression is broad enough to account for the multitude of experiences in different women's lives.

Jones is particularly interested in understanding how feminist theory can help us deal with Reformation understandings of sin and grace. She uses an example from Luther's theology of justification. In the first part of Luther's courtroom drama depiction of justification, God "crucifies" the arrogant self-assertion of the sinner who believes he is the center of the universe. The narcissistic exaltation is radically challenged and stripped away. This dethroning of the exalted self is the primary task of the law. According to Luther, this first attack on human pretense is necessary before one is ready to receive divine grace. Ego deflation, as William James would later put it, is the first step of the spiritual journey. For Luther, the Pelagian error of believing we can proudly resolve our own problem (without divine help) must be exposed before grace can be received.

In this courtroom imagery, Luther assumed a solid, strong-willed person in rebellion against his own limits. But Jones's question, once again, is whether or not this describes women's experience.

> What happens if feminist theology places this woman in the position
> of the sinner before God in Luther's courtroom drama? First, feminist
> theory helps us realize that this woman suffers from an illness different
> from Luther's classical sinner. Her sin is not one of overly rigid self-
> containment; her brokenness lies in her lack of containment, in her
> cultural definition in relation to others. Instead of an overabundance
> of self, the source of her alienation from God is her lack of self-defi-
> nition; she is too liquid, she lacks skin to hold her together, to em-
> brace and envelop her. She lacks the structuring boundaries that allow
> her to be an other in relationship to God in faith. She thus enters
> Luther's courtroom as a defendant already unraveled by the world, un-
> done by falsely inscribed relations to power. She comes not with a ro-

---

[21] Ibid., p. 71.

bust sense of self that needs to be dismantled by the wrath of the Law but as a de-centered subject whose lack of self is her prison.[22]

If this woman attempts to follow Luther's model, she may further denounce any emerging willfulness or assertiveness that would help her stand up against oppression. She is being invited to a passive role in her suffering. She forgets that this passivity is the very thing that contributes to her exploitation.

Thus, Jones, like Plaskow, Hampson, Ruether and others, believes it does little good to indict the male gender for everything that has gone wrong in Western civilization:

> Feminists contend that women are not only victims of these destructive forces but perpetuators as well. Feminists also assert that these forces of destruction are structural and hence larger than individual actions, and yet they still insist that individuals be held responsible for harms done and goods left undone, for oppressive forces unleashed and then left unchallenged. In other words, when analyzing forces of women's oppression, both persons and structures must be held culpable.[23]

The fact that "women's experience" is often unrelated to the prideful domination of the Western male ego does not mean that women are therefore free from sin.

SOCIAL VERSUS INDIVIDUAL SIN

Some feminists, as liberation theologians, see the Augustinian pride emphasis on personal or individual sin as a distraction from the real source of sin— the oppressive social structures that surround us. By excessively focusing on our private sin, we miss the interdependence of the human condition and the socioeconomic-ecological system in which we live. Sin is more of a structural, rather than an individual problem.

Yet astute feminist theologians recognize that while social structures indeed influence and shape human behavior, each of us participates and per-

---

[22]Jones, *Feminist Theory and Christian Theology*, pp. 62-63.
[23]Ibid., pp. 96-97.

petuates those social structures. We quietly contribute to the ongoing power of those structures. The relationship between our individual identity and those social forces is dialectical. We collectively create them, and they, in turn, further shape and mold us. Ruether believes we make a big mistake when we try to separate personal from systemic sin. They are instead intertwined.

> Sin always has a personal as well as a systemic side. But it is never just "individual"; there is no evil that is not relational. Sin exists precisely in the distortion of relationality, including relation to oneself. . . . The system is so much larger than the individual that one could easily imagine oneself totally helpless, the captive of demonic powers beyond one's control. Yet this system is the creation of humans, not of God or fallen angels. We made it. We perpetuate it by our cooperation with it. Without our many-sided cooperation with it, it could not continue to stand.[24]

Just as there is a danger in saying men and women are *biologically* hard wired to sin in different ways, so there is a danger in saying that we are *socially* determined to sin differently. Either way, freedom is lost as we are simply living out a destiny determined by factors outside the power of volition. The whole point of feminist consciousness raising is to say that awareness *can* bring change and that we are not locked into these roles. Determinism of the biological-essentialist variety or the social-constructivist variety needs to be avoided for there to be hope for change.

Standing up against the oppressive structures surrounding women will involve an inner strength that the "pride warning" may sabotage. Mary Stewart Van Leeuwen, in her *Gender and Grace*, puts this issue well. "If women insist on peace at any price—if they settle for abnormal quietism as a way of avoiding the risk and potential isolation that may result from opposing evil—then they are not exhibiting the fruit of the Spirit. They are sinning just as surely as the man who rides roughshod over relationships in order to assert his individual freedom."[25] Thus, it is important for women to

---

[24]Ruether, *Sexism and God-Talk*, pp. 181-82.
[25]Mary Stewart Van Leeuwen, *Gender and Grace* (Downers Grove, Ill.: InterVarsity Press, 1990), p. 46.

understand that trying to avoid a "male" version of sin (pride) may push them deeper into a "female" version of sin (unjust accommodation).

CONCLUSION

In spite of the depths of the Augustinian-Niebuhrian analysis of pride, feminist voices argue that there is another side to sin. They insist that by overemphasizing pride, the Augustinian tradition shortchanges the problems of self-avoidance.

What might Niebuhr or others in the Augustinian tradition say to these criticisms? Remember that they do not criticize the Augustinian tradition for being completely wrong about the human condition. Instead, feminist theologians have argued that the Augustinian tradition is simply limited, not inaccurate. It is particularly limited when describing the experience of women. Would Niebuhr nevertheless cling to his position that pride *is* the underlying issue, even in self-abnegation? Would he insist that all forms of distrusting God involve the process of God-replacement and, hence, prideful idolatry? Would Niebuhr say that even in the process of self-avoidance, we are still replacing God with our own "solutions" to the problem of anxiety and are therefore acting with pride? These are questions to be addressed in the last chapter, where we will search for a possible integration of the best of the Augustinian tradition and the important insights of feminist theologians.

Again, feminist theology argues that the Augustinian tradition is inaccurate on only one side of the genders, the female side. They do not raise the possibility that this tradition is wrong altogether. But what if the Augustinian tradition distorts the primary problem of both women and men? What if human sin and dysfunction cannot be attributed to the issue of pride? What if the problem of an undervalued self is primary, and the "pride diagnosis" does not get to the deeper layers of the human condition?

As previously noted, this non-Augustinian theme of an undervalued self runs throughout humanistic psychology. Carl Rogers is probably the best representative of this position. In fact, Rogers wants to invert Niebuhr's claim and argue that self-contempt is our most basic problem. We do not adequately accept and love ourselves. We now turn to his perspective.

SELF-ACCEPTANCE AND HUMANISTIC PSYCHOLOGY

If I were to search for the central core of difficulty in people as I have come to know them, it is that in the great majority of cases they despise themselves, regard themselves as worthless and unlovable. . . . I believe that only if one views individuals on the most superficial or external basis are they seen as being primarily the victims of self-love.
CARL ROGERS

The humanistic psychologies propose a different diagnosis of our primary problem than pride: an undervalued self. Humanistic psychology gladly parts company with the Augustinian tradition's rather somber estimate of the human condition. In fact, it frequently reverses the Augustinian-Niebuhrian interpretation: Instead of destructive behavior resulting from inordinate pride, pride is a cover-up for far deeper feelings of inadequacy and unworthiness. Pride, again, is never the central problem.

Humanistic psychology emerged in the mid-twentieth century as a reaction to both Freudian pessimism and behavioristic determinism. Tired of the psychoanalytic emphasis on pathology, humanistic psychology began focusing on what is healthy, rather than unhealthy, about human beings. Carl Rogers and Abraham Maslow were probably the two most important leaders in this new movement.

As I previously suggested, humanistic psychology frequently goes further than the feminist critique of the Augustinian pride thesis. While the feminist critique argues that Augustine and Niebuhr have not adequately described *women's* experience, humanistic psychologists, such as Carl Rogers, fault the Augustinian-Niebuhrian tradition for not describing *human* experience. While Rogers grants that human beings may appear full of pride, once we get to know them at a deeper level, we find something more complicated going on. So, like feminists, humanistic psychology rejects the dominant Augustinian-Niebuhrian strand in Christian thought. But it argues that the "pride model" is a misinterpretation of *both women and men*. Humanistic psychology asserts that the human organism has a basic drive or tendency toward growth and development rather than self-exaltation. This energetic thrust toward self-actualization needs only a nonthreatening atmosphere of trustworthiness in order to bloom. Social influences may distort and misguide this growth principle, but the organism can be healed in the context of a facilitative relationship. Low self-esteem is a definite problem; pride is not.

To some psychologists and many theologians this sounds entirely too much like the "everything is improving" mentality of the later nineteenth- and early twentieth-century liberal optimists. This naive notion of humanity's evolutionary progress, they argue, has been shattered by two world wars. In the aftermath of the Holocaust, how can anyone hold a positive view of human potential? In theology, the voice of Karl Barth dropped like a bombshell in the early part of the twentieth century and set the stage, along with Niebuhr and others, for a return to the more somber portrait of human nature in the Protestant Reformers. In addition, depth psychology pointed toward the vicious, destructive nature of unconscious instincts beneath our social pretentiousness. How could this humanistic optimism belong to the twentieth century?

Yet Carl Rogers, probably the best representative of humanistic psychology, grew accustomed to swimming upstream. He has had a controversial, even revolutionary, impact on the helping professions. In an essay entitled "Carl Rogers, Quiet Revolutionary," Richard Farson makes a strong statement concerning Rogers's influence:

> His work is basic to the restructuring of almost every field of human affairs. Consider some of the areas of influence. His ideas are the main ones used to support efforts toward democratic or participative man-

agement in industry. There has probably not been a single organizational development or management training program in twenty-five years which has not been built on his theoretical formulations. His ideas opened the way to student-centered teaching and learning and this philosophy of empowering the student contributed to the students' rights movement. His ideas cleared away the mystique of professionalism in psychiatry and the helping professions and gave impetus to the development and utilization of lay and paraprofessional resources and to dissident clergy unwilling to accept the hierarchical authority of the church. His ideas emphasized self-direction and personal responsibility in all the fields of health and welfare and helped spawn thousands of self-help groups.[1]

For decades, psychologists, social workers, psychiatric nurses, pastoral counselors, education leaders and practically every branch of the helping professions have been trained in skills that were largely developed by Rogers. Though Rogers's name has not always been mentioned, his ideas lie at the very core of terms like "attentive listening," "empathic understanding" and "reflection of feelings." These terms dominate the counseling process. He was the leading figure in helping open up psychotherapy to nonmedical practitioners. He is largely responsible for the supervised training of counseling students as part of their academic requirements. "Practicum training" is such a basic part of today's counseling programs that it is easy to forget it did not exist prior to Rogers. One may disagree with Rogers, even passionately reject some of his ideas, but it is historically irresponsible to refuse acknowledgment of his legacy in the helping professions. Discussing the history of counseling and psychotherapy in America without mentioning its indebtedness to Rogers is the equivalent of talking about theories of conditioning without mentioning B. F. Skinner.

Originally preparing for ministry, Rogers attended Union Theological Seminary in New York. Soon, however, he found theology too confining and migrated to psychology. The movement across the street from Union Theological Seminary to the psychology and education departments at

---

[1]Richard Farson, "Carl Rogers, Quiet Revolutionary," in *Carl Rogers: The Man and His Ideas,* by Richard Evans (New York: E. P. Dutton, 1975), pp. xl-xli.

Teachers College, Columbia University, symbolized much more than a walk across Broadway. Rogers describes his primary reason for this move:

> My own reason for deciding at that time to leave the field of religious work was that although questions as to the meaning of life and the possibility of the constructive improvement of life for individuals were of deep interest to me, I could not work in a field where I would be required to believe some specified religious doctrine. I realized that my own view had changed tremendously already and would very likely continue to change. It seemed to me that it would be a horrible thing to have to profess a set of beliefs in order to remain in one's profession. I wanted to find a field in which I could be sure my freedom of thought would not be limited.[2]

Little did Rogers realize at this time that he would later run into the same form of expected conformity and intellectual rigidity in the context of psychology departments also. He would rebel against those as well.

In order to understand Rogers's conviction that the Augustinian tradition has misled us with its emphasis on pride, it is necessary to understand the basic structure of his theory.

THE "GOSPEL" OF HUMANISTIC PSYCHOLOGY: THE ACTUALIZING TENDENCY

If there is one central element that undergirds all of humanistic psychology, it is a profound belief in the trustworthiness of what is called the "actualizing tendency." Rogers defines this actualizing tendency as "the inherent tendency of the organism to develop all its capacities in ways which serve to maintain or enhance the organism."[3] This involves far more than a striving for the basic needs of air, food, water and so on. It involves a movement toward autonomy and internal control as opposed to conformity to external standards.

---

[2]Carl Rogers, "Autobiography," in *A History of Psychology in Autobiography*, vol. 5, ed. E. G. Boring and G. Lindzey (New York: Appleton-Century-Crofts, 1967), pp. 354-55.

[3]Carl Rogers, "A Theory of Therapy, Personality, and Interpersonal Relationships as Developed in the Client-Centered Framework," in *Psychology: A Study of a Science*, vol. 3, *Formulations of the Person and the Social Context*, ed. S. Koch (New York: McGraw-Hill), p. 196.

It is important to recognize that this master motivation theory of self-actu-alization is *singularly,* rather than dually or multiply, oriented. Moreover, this is seen as a deeply rooted biological tendency. At base, we do not have multiple drives, but only one—a singular, unfolding pattern toward self-fulfillment. Rogers has always been very clear about this:"The organism has one basic ten-dency and striving—to actualize, maintain, and enhance the experiencing or-ganism"[4] And a very significant point for humanistic psychology is that this tendency does not involve a narcissistic, purely self-absorbed direction. Instead, it is a movement toward greater sociability and concern for others.

The formidable philosophical assumption here is that we each can be ut-terly trusted on our own growth journey, provided that we receive an ac-cepting, empathic invitation. We need no additional prompting, nudging or coercing. The actualizing tendency does not have a serious competitor. Rogers denies the Freudian death instinct, which Freud believed accompa-nied the life instinct. For Rogers, there is nothing essentially within us that pushes an opposing force of unhealthiness or destruction. The actualizing tendency is the basic, singular inclination of the "natural" person. In this sense, Rogers is very similar to Rousseau and others who argue that evil is always external to humanity's basic nature.[5] Nothing inherently within the organism threatens it. Destruction or cruelty is an outside-in maneuver, as the innocent organism is contaminated by forces within the family and so-cial order. If those negative influences could somehow be eliminated from organismic development, the individual, out of his or her own freedom, would consistently choose a healthy direction.

Nothing within the person provokes an ontological anxiety that can be destructive. While Rogers owes much to Kierkegaard, on this point he parts company with him. For Kierkegaard, as for Niebuhr, a profound tempta-tion arises within each of us (because of our finitude, insecurity and precar-ious position between nature and spirit) to engage in destructive behavior as we attempt to resolve our fundamental anxiety.[6] For Rogers, this internal

---

[4]Carl Rogers, *Client-Centered Therapy* (Boston: Houghton-Mifflin, 1951), p. 487.

[5]For an interesting account of Rogers's "blossoming self" as a continuation of Rousseau's romanticism, see Lawrence Kohlberg, "Development as the Aim of Education," *Harvard Educational Review* 42, no. 4 (1972): 449-95.

[6]Soren Kierkegaard, *The Concept of Anxiety,* trans. Reidar Thomte (Princeton, N.J.: Princeton University Press, 1980).

state does not pose a serious threat to the actualizing tendency. The only danger is external.

It is interesting to note here, once again, Rogers's radical differences with Freud. Far from believing that our most basic drives are primitive and dangerous, Rogers argues passionately that our innate tendency is to act in ways that are in the best interest of ourselves, as well as others. Browning puts it well: "Whereas Freud's model of constancy and death were based upon metaphors of inertia and resistance to growth, Rogers sees life, even the life of troubled and anxious people, through metaphors of forward movement, growth, and expansion."[7] For Freud, of course, the direct expression of the irrational and primitive drives would be disastrous. Socialization must salvage these brutal instincts from self-destruction for civilization to be possible. For Rogers, on the other hand, it is precisely those social pressures to conform that thwart the actualizing tendency. The inherent, natural direction of the human organism is quite trustworthy. It is the distortion of our natural state, rather than the expression of it, that is dangerous. Again, in Rogers's description of humanity, "the deepest characteristics tend toward development, differentiation, and cooperative relationships."[8]

So in Rogerian terms, pride, as the Augustinian tradition understands it, is not *natural* to us. Our natural inclination is appropriate self-regard, not inordinate self-regard. Our own existential anxiety does not tempt us toward self-exaltation. Our basic tendency is to value ourselves in a healthy way and, in turn, value others. It is only when this biologically motivated tendency toward appropriate self-valuation is frustrated by the environment that self-distortion and the undervaluing of self begin. We would never undervalue ourselves if it were not for external conditions of worth. We internalize these judgments and develop low self-esteem. Any appearance of pride is merely a mask for this deeper problem of self-disdain, and the distortions in our relationship with ourselves come from outside threats. Thus, self-deception, for Rogers, never emerges from our own ontological anxiety. On this issue, Rogers and Niebuhr fully disagree.

---

[7] Don Browning, *Religious Thought and the Modern Psychologies* (Philadelphia: Fortress, 1987), p. 66.
[8] Howard Kirschenbaum, *On Becoming Carl Rogers* (New York: Delta Books, 1979), p. 250.

"NATURAL GOODNESS":
THE ORGANISMIC VALUING PROCESS

Related to the actualizing tendency, the "organismic valuing process" is another important concept in Rogers's understanding of the self. In an article entitled "Toward a Modern Approach to Values: The Valuing Process in the Mature Person," he briefly sketches his view of this process.[9] He feels quite strongly that the infant is born with a steady approach to values. The infant clearly prefers some experiences while rejecting others. Roger believes that from studying an infant's behavior we can infer that the infant "prefers those experiences which maintain, enhance, or actualize the organism, and rejects those which do not serve this end."[10] An infant's approach is flexible and changing, a process rather than a rigid system.

The important point about infants' valuing process is that it occurs within themselves. They trust their own organism as the center of the valuing process. Rogers explains:

Unlike many of us, he *knows* what he likes and dislikes, and the origin of these value choices lies strictly within himself. He is the center of the valuing process, the evidence for his choices being supplied by his own senses. He is not at this point influenced by what his parents think he should prefer, or by what the church says, or by the opinion of the latest "expert" in the field, or by the persuasive talents of an advertising firm. It is from within his own experiencing that his organism is saying in non-verbal terms, "This is good for me." "That is bad for me." "I strongly dislike that." He would laugh at our concern over values, if he could understand it. How could anyone fail to know what he liked and disliked, what was good for him and what was not?[11]

Gradually, however, there is a retreat from this type of simple valuing. As infants learn that certain actions bring condemning judgments from others, they begin to replace their own sense of valuing with the introjected values

---

[9]Carl Rogers, "Toward a Modern Approach to Values: The Valuing Process in the Mature Person," in Carl Rogers and Barry Stevens, *Person to Person: The Problem of Being Human* (New York: Pocket Books, 1971).

[10]Ibid., p. 6.

[11]Ibid., p. 8.

of others—usually mom and dad. Infants completely dethrone an inner sense of trusting their own organism and place the locus of evaluation outside of themselves. Infants feel, of course, that they must behave according to an external set of values or they will not feel a part of a group. This sense of being loved hinges on adopting those external values.

For most people, once this internal valuing process is lost and replaced by an outsider's standard, it is never regained. In an effort to feel accepted, comfortable and even cared for, we accept external values. Rogers describes the change:

> In an attempt to gain or hold love, approval, esteem, the individual relinquishes the locus of evaluation which was his in infancy, and places it in others. He learns to have a basic *distrust* for his own experiencing as a guide to his behavior. He learns from others a large number of conceived values, and adopts them as his own, even though they may be widely discrepant from what his is experiencing. Because these concepts are not based on his own valuing, they tend to be fixed and rigid, rather than fluid and changing.[12]

As adults, many of us live in complete lack of awareness that most of our values are not of our own choosing but instead are handed down to us. In many cases, however, we become painfully aware of the discrepancy between our values and our experience. Often, rigid absolutes that have been given to us from an outside source may make little sense to our inner lives, yet we hold on to those external standards out of fear. We do not feel that we can trust the values that spring from within. In fact, because of this dilemma, we may find ourselves torn between conflicting values.

For Rogers, the therapy session offers a nonthreatening climate in which we can explore ourselves deeply and perhaps regain some of our internal valuing. In an atmosphere of empathy and trust, we can dare to *be* our feelings and perhaps come to trust a bit more of our inner wisdom. Rogers tries to help the client move toward a mature valuing process, obtaining outside evidence yet allowing one's values to develop from within. In many ways the valuing process of the mature adult is similar to the in-

---

[12]Ibid., p. 9.

fant's, yet the adult knowingly trusts his or her deep inner intuitions and feelings. Rogers makes the bold claim that when a person makes a free inward choice of values, that choice will be not only in the best interest of the self but in the best interest for the larger realm of society.[13] Regarding his profound trust in our ability to choose the most actualizing alternative, Rogers says, "I hypothesize that it is characteristic of the human organism to prefer such actualizing and socialized goals when he is exposed to a growth-promoting climate."[14]

INCONGRUENCE AND THE EMERGENCE OF THE UNDERVALUED SELF

Rather than pride or self-exaltation, Rogers believes the human dilemma revolves around "incongruence," acting inconsistently with our experiencing process. As we have seen, young children, born in a state of original congruence, fall into distorted awareness by trying to live up to conditions of worth imposed on them by adults. Having fallen into this state of distorted awareness (original sin?), individuals need help in reconnecting with their lost, but not destroyed, self-actualizing tendency. This innate tendency toward actualization has been thwarted by the abandoning of their own feelings in an attempt to accommodate to other people's expectations.

Thus, because we internalize these conditions of worth, we refuse to accept the full range of our experiencing process. It is at this moment that self-contempt is born. Because of the external rejection of part of ourselves, we too, reject those parts. Approval from the significant people in our lives (especially parents) is more important than the feelings, thoughts or experiences that do not match these outside standards. We become inwardly divided, with the unaccepted dimensions hated and condemned to darkness. We can pretend to be what outsiders expect. In this pretentious process, however, we will come to despise those aspects of ourselves that do not match this image. Thus, inward contempt is first "borrowed" from outsiders. Once borrowed, we then become quite efficient at self-depreciation, self-criticism and even self-hate. We hardly need any more outside help.

---

[13]Ibid., p. 19.
[14]Ibid.

This self-contempt can be very painful. In fact, it can be so hurtful that we mask it with a show of grandiosity, false confidence and arrogance. This display of pride, however, is always symptomatic of a deeper issue. Pride is never the primary diagnosis. Beneath the bravado is a person struggling with insecurity, a person dogged by self-doubt who creates a compensatory, exalted self.

Augustinian pride, then, for women *and* men, is always a secondary problem, not the primary one. The main problem is a lack of self-appreci- ation, a lack of self-value. In some cases, the self-contempt is direct and ob- vious. In other cases, however, low self-esteem may not directly present itself. Yet when the smoke screen of pride blows away, the undervalued self can be seen.

For Rogers and the humanistic psychologists, it is crucial that we recon- nect with our experiencing process. But this is frightening because our self- contempt threatens to condemn any self-discovery. Why should we explore feelings or thoughts that will only be further clobbered?

RECLAIMING THE DESPISED SELF

Reconnecting with the disowned, despised dimensions of our experience is pivotal for self-acceptance. Yet how do we do this? Rogers believes this is accomplished by recreating the conditions that needed to have been there from the beginning—the therapeutic triad of empathy, unconditional pos- itive regard and congruence. These Rogerian ingredients provide the non- threatening atmosphere by which defenses can be lowered and we can accept our own experiencing process. The disjunction between rigid self- concept and actual experience is softened as we become a more unified whole. Referring to Kierkegaard, Rogers frequently comments that the goal of therapy is "to be that self which one truly is."[15]

Rogers offers a well-developed theory of the core therapeutic conditions necessary for change to take place.[16] The first of these therapeutic ingredi- ents is empathy. Empathy is the process by which the therapist nonjudg- mentally enters the internal frame of reference of the client to understand

---

[15]Carl R. Rogers, *On Becoming a Person* (Boston: Houghton-Mifflin, 1961), p. 166.
[16]Ibid.

the "felt meaning" of the client's experience. Empathy seeks to help the client explore the frightening world of his or her own experience. It acceptantly embraces the client's frame of reference without conditions of worth, denial or diagnostic cleverness. This acceptance of the client's "interior design" does not necessarily mean that the therapist condones or approves of everything in the client's life. It means instead that the therapist is open to the full range of the client's experience without trying to censor, deny or minimize it. The therapist never loses his or her own identity in the empathic process.

The second core ingredient of effective therapy is unconditional positive regard, or an attitude of warmth, care and prizing of the client. The point is for the client to feel accepted and affirmed as a person of worth and value without performing or "doing" anything. In order for this quality to be consistently displayed, it must emerge out of a therapist's own philosophical orientation about human dignity. It is not simply a technique to employ; instead, it is an outgrowth of the therapist's deepest convictions about persons.

The third core ingredient, congruence, refers to the therapist's ability to be in touch with his or her own experiencing and to allow that process to be transparent in the relationship. Rogers describes this quality of congruence:

> I hypothesize that personal growth is facilitated when the counselor is what he *is,* when in the relationship with his client he is genuine and without "front" or facade, openly being the feelings and attitudes which at that moment are flowing in him. We have used the term "congruence" to try to describe this condition. By this we mean that the feelings the counselor is experiencing are available to him, available to his awareness, that he is able to live these feelings, be them in relationship, and able to communicate them if appropriate. It means that he comes into a direct personal encounter with his client, meeting him on a person-to-person basis.[17]

This quality of genuineness tends to be contagious. Put differently, congruence invites congruence. As the client sees that the therapist is willing to be real in the relationship, perhaps the client, too, can risk being open.

The evidence for the significance of the therapeutic triad has been very

---

[17]Ibid., p. 87.

well researched.[18] In fact, compared with other systems of psychotherapy, the research in client-centered therapy has been most impressive. Even in 1957, D. S. Cartwright reported over one hundred studies which had been done on the Rogerian system.[19] Many of these were doctoral dissertations. As early as 1940, Rogers used electrical recordings for his sessions. This was before tape recordings were even invented! In this process, perhaps no one has done as much to demystify the goings-on in a therapy session. Prior to Rogers, therapist recollections were used to remember the case, and therapy was largely clouded in mystery. Rogers wanted to open the process of therapy to investigation. Clearly, he put his own theory and therapy on the line in a way that required a great deal of courage.

"THEOLOGIZING" CARL ROGERS?

As I previously mentioned, many theological evaluations of Rogerian theory are critical of what they consider a naive, overly optimistic holdover from nineteenth-century progressivism.[20] They often see Rogers as a Pollyanna, a person who does not squarely face the problem of human evil.[21] Put theologically, he has an inadequate doctrine of sin.

The Augustinian theological tradition would accuse Rogers of failing to see the dangers of self-exaltation. Because Rogers minimizes the human capacity for sin, he holds an overly optimistic view of human potential. Rogers argues that people need to once again "believe in themselves"; Augustinians would argue that this excessive "belief in themselves," apart from God, is what got them in trouble in the first place.

---

[18]See Godfrey T. Barrett-Lennard, *Carl Rogers' Helping System: Journey and Substance* (London: Sage Publications, 1998), especially chaps. 12, 13 and 14. Barrett-Lennard's book is probably the most comprehensive study of Rogers available.

[19]Ibid.

[20]These perspectives vary in the intensity of their criticism. See James A. Oakland, "Self-Actualization and Sanctification," *Journal of Psychology and Theology* 2 (1974): 202-9; Harry Van Belle, *Basic Intent and Therapeutic Approach of Carl R. Rogers* (Toronto: Wedge Publishing, 1980); Robert C. Roberts, "Carl Rogers and the Christian Virtues," *Journal of Psychology and Theology* 13 (1985): 263-73; Doreen Dodgen and Mark R. McMinn, "Humanistic Psychology and Christian Thought: A Comparative Analysis," *Journal of Psychology and Theology* 14, no. 3 (1986): 194-202; and, of course, Paul Vitz, *Psychology as Religion: The Cult of Self-Worship* (Grand Rapids, Mich.: Eerdmans, 1994).

[21]This negative view of Rogers is challenged by Thomas C. Oden, *Kerygma and Counseling* (Philadelphia: Westminster Press, 1966); and by Don Browning, *Atonement and Psychotherapy* (Philadelphia: Westminster Press, 1966).

Rogers himself offers no explicit theological reflection after having left Union Seminary. In fact, his interest in theological questions seems to have turned completely to psychological ones. The break with the ministry seems as sharp and clear as his earlier break with his family's religion. It is not that Rogers simply rejected the fundamentalism of his childhood and youth. He was, after all, exposed at Union Theological Seminary to some of the most progressive theological minds in America. He sat through courses with people such as Harry Emerson Fosdick, who would have offered him a multitude of more liberal and progressive ways to rethink his own background. Thus, when Rogers replaced his focus in theology with psychology, he was turning away from liberal, as well as conservative, religious thought. Put simply, if he could not be comfortable with the liberal atmosphere at Union, it was clear that he would not feel at home in *any* theological atmosphere.

In spite of the misgivings of many theologians, Thomas Oden, especially in his early work, argues that it is quite possible to realistically "theologize" from a Rogerian framework.[22] Further, Oden argues that Rogers himself operates on the basis of an implicit ontological assumption about acceptance that is akin to the Christian tradition.[23]

Oden agrees with Rogers that all of us struggle mightily with feelings of unacceptability. Once a sense of internalized shame or unacceptability has occurred in us, we can't eliminate it on our own. We cannot solipsistically decide that we are okay and declare it so. After all, it is our own opinion that is in question, so why should we believe ourselves? A self-testimony means little when we are the very ones on trial.

So what do we need? We need the accepting understanding of another person who is able to nonjudgmentally enter our frame of reference and mediate to us our acceptability. Oden believes this is an act of grace. Why? Because an accepting therapist is not just communicating that he or she, as a therapist, accepts us. Nor is the accepting therapist saying, as a representative of society, that the community accepts us. No, the therapist is saying something much more powerful than that. The therapist is saying, in effect,

---

[22] Oden, *Kerygma and Counseling.*
[23] Ibid.

that *we* are acceptable—period! We are acceptable, not just to the therapist, and not just to the community, but to life itself. Our essence is acceptable.

This is an ontological message about the nature of reality itself. This is not simply an anthropological or humanistic assumption, but a tacit theological assumption about the nature of being. The therapist does not arrive at this belief as a result of empirical investigation or rational deduction. It is, simply put, an assumption, a philosophical premise, a first principle that makes therapy possible. It must be assumed from the beginning. The very Source of life accepts us. Anything that tells us we are flawed, defective or unacceptable is not speaking the truth.

A therapist may have no idea that he or she is speaking, implicitly, as a theologian. Yet for Oden, insofar as the therapist mediates a message about the very structures of reality, he or she can be a mediator of grace. And insofar as the client embraces this message of acceptability, even when there is not one word of explicit religious language uttered, the client experiences the grace of God. Later, the client may come to realize the larger, cosmic significance of this encounter. Yet God's name does not have to be employed for God's grace to be experienced.

Don Browning's important early work *Atonement and Psychotherapy* also emphasizes how the therapist points toward a reality of acceptance that is much larger than what is going on between therapist and client. He states that "the therapist's empathic acceptance announces, proclaims, and witnesses to the fact that the client is truly acceptable," not just to the therapist but to a transcendent power, and that "the client does not come to feel that he is acceptable simply to the therapist, but accepts the fact that he is acceptable in an ontological sense."[24] Browning suspects that it is this "broader context of meaning" that makes therapy successful. "Successful therapy rests upon a *generalization* of an experience the client has with the therapist. The fact that the therapist may never name this larger structure does not negate the fact that his attitude implies it."[25] Thus, some of the most powerful encounters with acceptance may occur in a therapist's office. Divine presence often works quietly and behind the scenes. Rogers, or any other person

---

[24]Don Browning, *Atonement and Psychotherapy*, pp. 150-51.
[25]Ibid.

communicating unconditional acceptance, acts as a representative (minister?) of the accepting reality of God. Implicitly, Rogers communicates a message of acceptance whose source is beyond the empirical world. He mediates ontological acceptance.

Oden points out that unless this "accepting reality" has made itself known to us, however, we can never really know that we are ontologically acceptable. The Christian proclamation announces that this accepting reality has made itself known to us in a historical event. In other words, this vague assumption in secular psychotherapy is the declaration of the gospel, the announcement that God prizes us in the midst of our distorted existence. The purpose of preaching is to bring us to the awareness of the reality of the situation in which we already stand. Regardless of what we may think or feel about our human condition, in reality, we are already loved and accepted by God. Following Karl Barth, Oden thinks the gospel proclaims that we should "be who we are" as accepted persons.[26] In fact, sin is a failure to be who we really are, a refusal to accept our true identity as we live outside the awareness that we are the accepted children of God. Oden thus argues that sin is, more than anything else, living a lie.[27] He describes how the gospel message challenges this lie:

> The good news, Emmanuel, that God is with us and for us, which is the implicit basis of counseling, is the explicit basis of preaching: You are accepted not of your own initiative but in fact whether you accept it or not, and called to accept your acceptability. You are elected by God's love whether or not you receive and affirm your election. You are the son of the Father no matter to what extent you take your inheritance and flee to a far country.[28]

Thus, for Oden, the ontological status of humanity is forgiven even though we may be living miles away from this awareness. Oden therefore distinguishes universal election (God's unconditional acceptance of each of us) from universal salvation (our appropriation of that reality).[29] The tragedy

---

[26] Oden, *Kerygma and Counseling.*

[27] For a fuller development of this theme, see Karl Barth, *Church Dogmatics,* 3/4 and 4/1 (Edinburgh: T & T Clark, 1961, 1956).

[28] Oden, *Kerygma and Counseling,* p. 26.

[29] Oden, *Structure of Awareness,* p. 104.

is that much of humanity lives as if we are not forgiven. Many of us, then, are strangers to our own condition, unaware that we are accepted.

An interesting point for Oden is that confession is not a prerequisite for receiving pardon. God's forgiveness both logically and psychologically precedes our ability to confess or repent. "It is only amid a community of genuine acceptance where unconditional forgiveness is mediated that persons find the freedom to put down their self-righteous defenses and freely enter into a responsible covenant relation with their neighbors."[30] Oden suggests that this affirmation of forgiveness preceding repentance surprises us "only because we have read the biblical witness with systematic blinders to the unconditional, universal scope of divine forgiveness and implicitly assumed that God's pardon is wholly contingent upon our acceptance of it."[31] This point seems central to psychotherapy. It is as clients find themselves accepted that they can dare to look within. Grace is the forerunner of introspection. Without an assurance in advance, the journey within is simply too frightening. Every therapist knows that clients will only delve deeply within themselves when they know it is safe. Otherwise, the findings could be devastating. Acceptance helps fuel the inward journey.

In a fascinating chapter of *Kerygma and Counseling* titled "The Theology of Carl Rogers," Oden attempts to smoke out the hidden theological themes in Rogers's thought.[32] He says that if by theology we mean a "deliberate and systematic attempt to speak self-consistently of man's predicament, redemption, and authenticity, then the therapeutic work of Carl Rogers has deep theological concerns, even though he has little to say formally about God."[33] Oden's task is not to simply translate Rogers's psychological terms into theological ones but to show, at an implicit level, that Rogers is already functioning as a theologian. Oden examines Rogers from the three-fold structure of (a) humanity's predicament, (b) redemptive possibilities for deliverance from that predicament and (c) a way of continuing growth in the new reality of that redemption.[34] He believes this structure

---

[30]Oden, *Structure of Awareness*, p. 117.
[31]Ibid., p. 117.
[32]Oden, *Kerygma and Counseling*, chap. 3.
[33]Ibid., p. 83.
[34]Ibid., p. 84.

corresponds to the traditional theological arrangement of sin, grace and authenticity, and that he is not supplying a mere theological overlay to psychological terms, but that Rogers is already functioning as a theologian, whether Rogers acknowledges it or not.

Interestingly, though Rogers officially left the world of ministry, he has had an enormous impact on the field of pastoral counseling. In a survey of pastoral counseling literature, Oden found that Rogers was second only to Freud in terms of number of references.[35] As Oden reminds us, "There is undoubtedly a deep subsoil of Christian devotion underneath his entire empathetic orientation, which cannot be ignored if one looks seriously at the direction of his whole career of vocational service."[36]

Let's begin with humanity's "original condition." Oden insists that Rogers has a strong "doctrine" of humanity's goodness *(imago Dei)* as well as humanity's fallenness and estrangement (sin).[37] For Rogers, as we have seen, the human infant enters the world in a state of congruence with a complete lack of phoniness, self-deception and self-estrangement. There is a smooth continuity between behavior and what is going on within the infant. Experience is not distorted by anxious defenses. There is an innocent quality of genuineness about the infant. This is the symbolic Garden of Eden. This is a world prior to any form of self-alienation. Here the full possibilities of the good life are present. Oden puts it this way:

> Although Rogers, of course, has no such view of man's primordial condition, or the will of God as the end of authentic self-actualization, nevertheless his emphatic insistence upon the inviolability of the self-actualizing tendency can be viewed as a secularized way of speaking of the persistent impulse in man toward authenticity, a way similar, despite differences, to the inviolability of the *imago Dei*.[38]

Eden, then, is this developmental condition full of possibility. Although conditions of worth and the fallen world or incongruence are bound to follow, this is the state of purity and goodness. So what happens?

---

[35]Thomas Oden, *Care of Souls in the Classical Tradition* (Philadelphia: Westminster Press, 1984), p. 31.
[36]Oden, *Kerygma and Counseling*, p. 85.
[37]Ibid., p. 88.
[38]Ibid., p. 90.

Rogers's "fall" is a developmental one. As we have seen, the infant, fully equipped with the possibilities of organismic valuing, eventually comes face-to-face with external "conditions of worth." This unfortunate, and inevitable, process involves the introjection of external values in such a manner that our own experience is distorted. The self begins to lose touch with its own concrete experiencing process and becomes a "stranger" to many of its own feelings.

Oden speaks of this process as a "fall from organismic experiencing," in which "one is forced to leave the Eden of the neonate situation . . . and is cast out into the alien land of incongruence, in which there is a disjunction between selfhood and experience."[39] The child, who had previously trusted his or her own organismic valuing process, now develops self-distrust.

Often, a rigid self-concept based on what we think others will accept operates independently of what we really think, feel and perceive. We have "lost ourselves" in that we no longer know what we want, need, value or even love. We quite literally do not know ourselves anymore. That creative, trustworthy actualizing tendency has been abandoned, and we live in a state of distorted awareness. Our image of self and our actual experience are at odds with each other.

Incongruence involves us in endless attempts at self-justification. We become preoccupied with trying to meet particular conditions of worth that might grant us legitimation. Browning elaborates on this issue of justification, saying that incongruence stems from the self's efforts "to render itself worthy and acceptable. It is precisely the character of the incongruent person to believe that his existence is justified only under certain conditions. . . . This attempt to justify oneself through one's conditions of worth is always a matter of absolutizing something finite and relative."[40] This absolutizing of a particular condition of worth invariably becomes idolatrous. It is the god by which we seek justification. In vain, we attempt to find acceptance before a finite deity that leaves us feeling rejected.

Rogers also describes what theologians have traditionally called a "bondage of the will." He acknowledges that one of the most difficult aspects of

---

[39]Ibid., p. 90-91.
[40]Browning, *Atonement and Psychotherapy*, p. 108.

self-estrangement is that we don't even realize that we are estranged. Acting out of the many defenses erected to protect the false self, we live in a state of darkness concerning the severity of our dilemma. Put theologically, sin blocks its own discovery. The rigid, recalcitrant self stonewalls actual experience. Defenses insidiously convince us that what we really feel is not real. It is out of this self-alienated state that we do vicious things to self and others. Rogers states his position bluntly: "I would not want to be misunderstood on this. I do not have a Pollyanna view of human nature. I am quite aware that out of defensiveness and inner fear, individuals can and do behave in ways which are incredibly cruel, horribly destructive, immature, regressive, anti-social, hurtful."[41]

Endless and fruitless attempts at self-justification are a part of this bondage. Like a person in quicksand, the more we attempt to nail down acceptance, the deeper we go into self-doubt and self-alienation. Recognizing the gap between our self-concept and our actual experience produces enormous anxiety. After all, we could be in danger of having to change the way we perceive ourselves. That's far too threatening. Consequently, internal violence is done as the "dangerous" feelings or experiences are eliminated. Having grown accustomed to this internal violence to self, it is then much easier to be violent with others. Anxious about the possibility of altering our self-definition, our defenses reinforce our incongruence, and we continue to be strangers to ourselves. Oden describes the relationship of incongruence and sin:

> If *sin* (*hamartia* in the New Testament) means missing the mark of one's authentic self, then surely Rogers' analysis of the dynamics of incongruence constitutes a rich explication and fresh restatement of the doctrine of sin. Absent, of course, is the broader Christian interpretation which argues that man's self-estrangement is more deeply interpreted as estrangement from the ground of his being. Although Rogers says little along these lines, his analysis of the human predicament does not preclude such an elaboration, and in fact it can be argued, invites such an analysis. Of course, Rogers, for good reasons

---

[41]Rogers, *On Becoming a Person*, p. 27.

eschews such terms as sin, which lend themselves to a moralistic dilu-
tion of the human predicament, but the depth dimension of the human quandary is not thereby diminished in his theory of therapy.[42]

Thus, Rogers's developmental and phenomenological description of incongruence leads toward an ontological discussion of humanity's condition in
relation to its Source.

So what is the way out of this bondage? How do we find deliverance from
this self-preoccupied attempt at justification? For Rogers, we do not have
the ability to grant ourselves acceptance. This is not something we can accomplish on our own. A disrupted relationship led to our estrangement with
self; a healed relationship is essential for our recovery. In this respect, Rogers
certainly does not offer a do-it-yourself form of secular salvation. We cannot
dredge up ontological acceptance out of the depths of our own psyches.
Healing is, of necessity, relational. As already noted, if a deep sense of inadequacy has convicted us and placed us on trial, then our own testimony on
behalf of ourselves is not enough. Somehow, our acceptance must be mediated, reflected from the depths of an interpersonal bridge with another.

To mediate acceptance to another first requires that we enter into the
other's internal frame of reference. This involves the careful journey into another person's private world of experience and meaning. Genuine media-
tors of acceptance must be willing to stand with others in their internal
landscape. Feelings that seem bizarre, shameful, horrible, evil or embarrass-
ing must be recognized and acknowledged. As Oden puts it, the mediator
of acceptance "engages in a certain kind of descent into hell, the hell of the
internal conflict of the estranged man, a kenosis, an incarnate participation
of the suffering of his human brother."[43]

Using a Barthian analogy of faith, Oden reads this interpersonal process
through the lens of God's empathic entry into our world of distorted awareness (incarnation). This cosmic declaration of our acceptance illumines the
interpersonal process of healing. Understood this way, it is not the therapist
or nonjudgmental friend who is the creator of our acceptability. The therapist or friend merely reflects a reality that is ontological—built into the

---

[42]Oden, *Kerygma and Counseling*, pp. 94-95.
[43]Ibid., p. 95.

very structure of reality. God has chosen to unconditionally love, value and prize us in the midst of our value distortion, estrangement and bondage. This acceptance, ultimately grounded in God's activity in Christ, is what liberates us from this predicament. The therapist or friend merely points toward the reality in which we already stand. Thus, an analogy of faith views this interpersonal process as grace incognito:

> Thus at the center of Rogers' theology stands a strong soteriology (doctrine of salvation), which argues that when certain conditions are present, the resolution of the human predicament occurs, or at least can occur. Therapy does not consist in the proclamation of these conditions, but of the concrete mediation of them through a relationship that frees the self to be itself. . . . In this relationship the reality of acceptance must be made transparently real to the anxious and defensive individual. Only when the congruent neighbor can dwell for a time in the private world of the fragmented man without judgment or evaluation, mediating an attitude of warmth, interest, respect, care, concern, and understanding, unconditionally prizing each fluctuating facet of the individual's self-expression and consciousness as it reveals itself, only then is the demonic power of human estrangement broken.[44]

Oden is quick to point out that the mediation of this saving event is never merely a concept. The idea of our acceptance is not healing until it is concretely embodied in a relationship in which we actually experience it. The simple thought that there is some sort of external reality that accepts us is not enough to combat the onslaught of rejecting voices in our lives. Instead, this acceptance must be experienced in the belly, not just thought about with the head.

As the estranged person receives this ontological word of acceptance relayed by a therapist or friend, he or she is then free to acknowledge discrepancies between the real and false self. Faults can be admitted without a pulverizing sense of rejection. The backdrop of acceptance allows a person to look more deeply within. Whatever is found, there is far less need to be defensive because the estranged person has *experienced* the liberating message

---

[44]Ibid., pp. 97-98.

of acceptance. The entire "self" is no longer on trial. Since the verdict of acceptance is already in, the individual can get on with life without the devastating self-preoccupation that grows out of rigid defensiveness. Like persons walking a tightrope with the knowledge that there is a safety net beneath, we are freed from the paralyzing anxiety of making a fatal mistake. The full range of experience and feelings can be admitted without necessarily acting on them. Self-acceptance follows as a result of being accepted. We are able to love because we have been loved. Put theologically, this is an experience of growth in grace or sanctification. The goal of sanctification is perfection; the goal of growth for Rogers is the fully functioning person. In both cases, these are ongoing processes rather than static states. Moreover, like traditional Christian theology, "Rogers' theology goes the full circle, . . . from the original situation of man as open to himself, the fall of man into incongruence, the saving event of unconditional positive regard, and the growth of man toward a full functioning which is similar to the original situation of man prior to the fall."[45]

A therapeutic relationship, then, can be a powerful example of God's grace at work incognito. A therapist can be free to operate with a Rogerian methodology while seeing the deeper picture of ontological acceptance. This interpersonal process of grace can then be further clarified by celebrating its reality in a community of faith. God's *yes* to humanity, communicated through therapeutic acceptance and the incognito Christ, can then be explicitly understood as the reality in which we stand.

In spite of his early eagerness to dialogue with humanistic psychology, however, Oden realizes that there are limitations to Rogerian thought. He does not naively embrace Rogers without a critical assessment. For instance, Oden thinks Rogers is in dire need of a larger framework for understanding the therapeutic process. If Rogers communicates the client's fundamental acceptability, then who, exactly, is doing the accepting? If it is merely Rogers, then the client can easily find a rejecting voice soon after he or she leaves the counseling session. Will this, then, cancel out the acceptance of the therapist's single voice? Stated differently, if Rogers claims that the very essence or being of the client is acceptable, then that is a heavy

---

[45]Ibid., p. 105.

philosophical assumption that needs elaboration. If we push the therapeutic insight, it raises a much larger question about the Source of being.[46]

Thus, the interpersonally accepting community of therapy needs a more explicit theological understanding of the Ground of that acceptance. Grace, after all, is not simply an experience without a source. Interpersonal discussions of grace must eventually point toward a divine reality. As humans, we can point toward grace, sometimes model and communicate it, but we cannot create it. That is the job of the Giver of life.

For Oden, the language of the historic Christian tradition is crucial because it announces the divine acceptance of humanity, an explicit message that undergirds Rogers's ability to communicate the client's value and acceptability. This is the primary function of the church, namely, to celebrate the reality of divine acceptance. This fuller understanding of our accepted status before our Creator expands and enriches our understanding of interpersonal acceptance:

> The therapeutic process limits itself strictly to the assumption that some accepting reality is being mediated through a special interpersonal relationship, without braving the question of the source of acceptance as a fundamental question of being. . . . Consequently Rogers develops a soteriology without a Christology, i.e., view of the saving process without a historical event which once for all manifests and defines that saving process and gives the history of salvation a center in time and space. It is a humanistic soteriology without any acknowledged celebration of God's act, God's acceptance, God's unconditional positive regard.[47]

Oden is not saying here that Rogers's psychotherapy is therefore debilitated. Instead, he is saying that it needs to recognize and acknowledge the ontological situation in which it stands, namely, that it is undergirded by the acceptance of God, the very Source of reality. While God hardly needs to be named in order for healing to occur, and while grace often works incognito, what most fulfills us is the further act of consciously celebrating

---

[46]Ibid., p. 109.
[47]Ibid., p. 111.

this divine reality in an explicit theological understanding.

Oden helps us understand that a theological reading of Rogers can help enrich our understanding of the dynamics of sin. The frantic attempt to win acceptance from the conditions of worth in our lives exposes the futility of all attempts to establish our acceptance apart from God's grace. Finite acceptance, no matter how hard we chase it, will never meet our heart's insecurity. However, Rogers's discussion of incongruence and the condition of self-estrangement needs a fuller development of the self in relation to God. Ultimately, sin is a theological problem before it is a psychological problem. Disturbed intrapsychic and interpersonal relationships indicate a disturbance in our relationship with our Creator. In this sense, secular psychology can greatly aid us in seeing the human ramifications of sin, but it fails to properly understand sin's ultimate cause. Sin is first and foremost a rupture in our relationship with God. No attempt to psychologize sin, without facing this root problem, will prove effective.

It is important here to briefly mention a point I will take up more fully in the final chapter. Perhaps humanistic psychology and the Augustinian tradition see the issue of pride so differently because one group is looking at pride strictly as a psychological issue (humanistic psychology) whereas the other group is seeing pride as primarily a theological issue. But is it possible for the psychological issue of low self-esteem to be based on the theological issue of pride? In other words, is it possible that the interpersonal appearance of low self-esteem could be based on a distrust in our Source and, hence, an implicit pride in our own human attempts to reach absolute security? We may well find that in the Augustinian tradition, particularly in Niebuhr, distrust of God and pride are two sides of the same process. Insofar as we rely on our own attempts to outmaneuver our anxiety, apart from dependence on God, we commit the sin of pride. It may not look like the kind of puffed-up pride we are used to seeing. Yet for Niebuhr, all refusal to trust God is based on a pride in our own solutions to the problem of being human.

PRIDE AND LOW SELF-ESTEEM INTERTWINED?

Perhaps we should again raise the question, how do people get so down on themselves? Rogers has given us his reason: we internalize other people's expectations and harshly judge ourselves. But is there something more to it than that? Could there be an element of pride involved in the production of low self-esteem? Is low self-esteem a result of prideful efforts to meet some standard of acceptability apart from a relationship in God? As Browning puts it, "Sin is man's attempt to find both the source of life and the justification of life in something other than his relationship with God."[48]

Before I revisit Niebuhr and the Augustinian tradition, I want to ask whether any psychological theory understands both pride and self-contempt as part of the human dilemma. Rather than one preceding the other, could they occur simultaneously? In other words, while Rogers has insisted that low self-esteem underlies displays of pride, is there any sense in which pride may be behind displays of low self-esteem? Where one is in the foreground, is the other in the background? Could both experiences be part of a singular process? Must we pick one over the other, or say that one *causes* the other?

The connection between pride and self-contempt appears to be more complex and paradoxical than we may have first imagined. To explore this issue further, we will examine the work of a woman who spent much of her life trying to grasp the relationship between pride and self-contempt. She is the neo-Freudian personality theorist and analyst Karen Horney. At times, Horney writes about the issue of pride as if she is planted in the Augustinian-Niebuhrian tradition. At other times, she writes about the issue of self-contempt as if she is a Rogerian. Her perspective, to which I now turn, offers rich insight toward a comprehensive understanding of sin.

---

[48]Browning, *Atonement and Psychotherapy*, p. 35.

6

PRIDE AND SELF-HATE:
TWO SIDES OF THE
SAME COIN?

Pride and self-hate belong inseparably together;
they are two expressions of one process.
KAREN HORNEY

Thus far, we have seen that both excessive pride and low self-esteem often describe the human condition. We have examined the Augustinian-Niebuhrian conviction that pride is primary, the feminist objection that pride does not describe women's experience and the humanistic psychology position that pride does not adequately account for anyone's experience. For humanistic psychology, if pride emerges, it is a false front designed to protect an undervalued self. Along the way, we have occasionally hinted at the possibility that this pride versus self-contempt debate may not be an either-or question after all.

It is my conviction that the work of neo–Freudian analyst Karen Horney offers promise in dealing with our deadlock between the overvalued and undervalued self. It is important to understand her treatment of the pride/self-contempt dichotomy before we move into the final chapter, which explores possibilities for integrating both views.

Horney's discussion of basic anxiety, the "idealized self," the "tyranny of the should," the "pride system" and the nature of self-hate all point toward the intertwined relationship between neurotic pride and self-contempt. Her insights are crucial for understanding how a vulnerable, insecure self underlies an arrogant appearance. But her perspective is also valuable in understanding how a neurotic pride system underlies an appearance of self-contempt and low self-esteem. Put simply, she points toward the insecurity in pride and the pride in insecurity. Horney's work has largely gone untapped in helping develop a Christian understanding of the dynamics of sin. It is the purpose of this chapter to explore her work with an eye toward how pride and self-contempt may both be part of one process, rather than polar opposites.

From 1932 until 1934, Horney was the director of the Chicago Psychoanalytic Institute. At that point she moved to New York, where she established a private practice and taught at the New York Psychoanalytic Institute. While in New York, Karen developed connections with an outstanding group of social scientists that included such names as Erich Fromm, Harry Stack Sullivan, Margaret Mead, Ruth Benedict and others. It was here that, in 1937, she officially divorced her husband, after they had been separated for quite some time. She continued to challenge orthodox Freudian theory, which raised the eyebrows of some members of the New York Psychoanalytic Institute. She eventually resigned and helped found the American Institute of Psychoanalysis as a means of promoting many of her own theories. She died of cancer in 1952.

In many respects, much of Karen Horney's life involved a struggle with authoritarian men. Clearly, her father was an authoritarian who favored Karen's older brother over her and tended to minimize any of Karen's academic dreams. Then, Oscar, her husband, was so similar to her father that it is easy to speculate on how she was still trying to deal with "father issues" in her marriage. And finally, her involvement in psychoanalysis represented another authority figure, Freud himself, who seemed to forbid the development of her own ideas. Themes of inferiority, competition, arrogance, compensation and revenge inevitably found their way into her exceedingly insightful view of the human condition. And in my view, the central accomplishment of her work is a portrayal of the intricate connection between an overvalued and undervalued self.

BASIC ANXIETY

Much like Niebuhr's, Horney's view of the self begins with what she frequently calls "basic anxiety." By this term, she means "the feeling a child has of being isolated and helpless in a potentially hostile world."[1] Also like Niebuhr, she believes that while this anxiety is not inherently destructive, it is the precondition of neurotic behavior. The child is extremely vulnerable to the threats of the immediate environment. Horney lists some of the specific dangers that arouse excessive anxiety:

> A wide range of adverse factors in the environment can produce this insecurity in a child: direct or indirect domination, indifference, erratic behavior, lack of respect for the child's individual needs, lack of real guidance, disparaging attitudes, too much admiration or the absence of it, lack of reliable warmth, having to take sides in parental disagreements, too much or too little responsibility, over-protection, isolation from other children, injustice, discrimination, unkept promises, hostile atmosphere, and so on and so on.[2]

A particular element affecting a child is a sense of "lurking hypocrisy" in the parents' attitude toward him or her. The parents' love and generosity may not be real. This suspicion that the parents' affection for the child may not be completely genuine is similar to Rogers's understanding of the "conditions of worth" placed on the child. The child does not have the unconditional security desired.

In her earlier work, Horney refers to anxiety as primarily an interpersonal problem. This emphasis on interpersonal anxiety sounds much like Rogers and humanistic psychology. In her later work, however, she is more interested in intrapsychic anxiety. In other words, she develops a greater concern for the anxiety resulting from one's relationship to oneself. In this concern, she sounds more like Niebuhr.

THREE NEUROTIC TRENDS TO
ALLEVIATE ANXIETY

As an outgrowth of basic anxiety, a child develops patterns of relating to

---

[1]Karen Horney, *Our Inner Conflicts* (New York: W. W. Norton, 1945), p. 41.
[2]Ibid.

other people that are designed to reduce interpersonal anxiety. The more anxious we become, the more rigidly we cling to a particular pattern. Horney identifies three patterns, or what she calls "neurotic trends." She describes these as interpersonal "movements": (1) moving against others, or the self-expansive solution, (2) moving toward others, or the self-effacing solution and (3) moving away from others, the resignation solution. Moving against others emphasizes hostility; moving toward others accents helplessness; and moving away from others highlights detachment. Each of these interpersonal trends represents a way to solve the anxiety of how to relate to other people. Let's look at each of these anxiety "solutions" in more detail.

   1. *Moving against others: the self-expansive solution.* Moving against others is an attempt to alleviate interpersonal anxiety by conquering, defeating and dominating others. An excessive need to control one's surroundings is typical of this trend. Pride or excessive self-regard seems dominant. Strength, leadership, heroism and omnipotence are prized. Horney refers to this trend as the self-expansive solution. It is based on an exaggerated need to master everything in one's life. A "conquest mentality" is typical as dominance, authoritarianism and vindictive triumph are deeply valued. This perspective places a premium on intelligence and will power, while it pushes away the world of feelings. Its greatest fear is helplessness, which it must repress at all costs. There is a rigid, compulsive need to eliminate self-doubts or any form of self-accusation. This denial of all self-doubt is crucial in maintaining the subjective conviction of superiority. Enormous energy goes into ignoring any possibility of failure. Any form of self-criticism is avoided. Similarly, being fooled, conned or deceived would bring a devastating injury to one's pride system. Self-expansive persons are most proud of their keen power of observation and ability to "call a spade a spade."

   Horney outlines three major types in the self-expansive, moving-against-others group. The first is narcissism, which she calls "being in love with one's idealized image. More precisely, the person is his idealized self and seems to adore it."[3] This appears as self-confidence, though it really is not. Consciously, these individuals may have no self-doubts. They may seem to have an unquestioned belief in their own greatness and strength. They may also appear charm-

---

[3]Ibid., p. 194.

ing. Yet they need endless confirmation of their superiority. As Horney describes the narcissist, "His feeling of mastery lies in his conviction that there is nothing he cannot do and no one he cannot win."[4] Narcissists may even appear loving and generous, but they always anticipate the flattery and praise they will later receive. They can also withstand jokes about themselves as long as the jokes bring them further attention and their image is not seriously questioned.

A sense of entitlement is another major feature of narcissists. They expect to be loved unconditionally no matter how they behave. If they have regularly trespassed on the rights of others, they expect total forgiveness without making any sort of amends. The idea that others may expect something from them or offer them *any* criticism sends them into a deep resentment, often with an accompanying outburst of fury. If they do not express rage, narcissists may sink into the depths of despair. Again, all criticism is perceived as an outrageous injustice, utterly devastating to the grandiose self.

The second subdivision of the moving-against-others, self-expansive type comprises the perfectionists. Instead of completely identifying with their inflated image (as the narcissist does), these perfectionists identify with their superior standards of behavior. While perfectionists condescendingly look down on others, their arrogant contempt for others is often hidden. According to Horney, even perfectionists often fail to recognize the manner in which they hold others in contempt because of shortcomings. Much of this is, of course, the projection of their own unconscious self-contempt.

Perfectionists differ from narcissists in that their primary goal is gaining others' respect, rather than their worship. Perfectionists would discount excessive flattery anyway. Horney indicates that the perfectionists' beliefs in their greatness are less naive than the narcissists, yet perfectionists, too, have an inflated expectation for complete justice. In other words, they are entitled to fair treatment in life because of their high standards. After all, they are fair, just and dutiful, so how dare life not also contain an infallible justice! According to Horney, perfectionists hate all undeserved fortune, regardless of whether it is good or bad. This "invalidates the whole accounting system."[5] Perfectionists tend to be letter-of-the-law people, even

---

[4]Ibid.
[5]Ibid., p. 197.

when they unconsciously know they do not live up to this standard. Any notion of grace, or unmerited favor, seems extremely suspicious to them. People are in charge of their own destinies and, hence, get what they deserve. Having perfectionist standards thus provides two important elements: (a) being superior to others and (b) controlling life.

The third subdivision in the expansive solution Horney calls arrogant vindication. These individuals have an overwhelming need for vindictive triumph. In fact, vindication, or vengeance, becomes an entire way of life. This compulsive need for vindication is often accompanied by extreme competitiveness. They want to intimidate others into a subdued position. In describing the hypercompetitiveness of this anxiety "solution," Horney says, "As a matter of fact he cannot tolerate anybody who knows or achieves more than he does, wields more power, or in any way questions his superiority. Compulsively he has to drag his rival down or defeat him."[6] Perhaps the most noticeable expression of this vindictive competition is violent rage. Even a hint that someone else might be superior brings on a fury. Horney frequently refers to this as being "seized by vindictive wrath."

Connected with this hypercompetitiveness, arrogant-vindictive persons are highly suspicious of hospitable gestures. These friendly behaviors are interpreted as covertly manipulative and malevolent. Therefore, any offer of help must stem from crooked motives. Or, friendliness may be simply perceived as stupidity.

The reality is that those engaged in this type of vindictive competition often want to humiliate their opponents. They frequently have a severe insensitivity toward others, and if others object to this callous treatment, then those objections are interpreted as weakness, being "too sensitive" or "touchy-feely." However it is put, the idea is that all feeling-oriented people are neurotically sensitive and had better toughen up if they are going to make it in this highly competitive world; vindictive individuals assume that others are as cutthroat as they are.

Vindictive triumph always necessitates being the invincible master of every situation. These persons demand to have their neurotic needs met and feel entitled to disregard others' needs. The vindictive person "feels entitled

---

[6]Ibid., p. 198.

for instance to the unabridged expression of his unfavorable observations and criticisms but feels equally entitled to never to be criticized himself. He is entitled to decide how often or how seldom to see a friend and what to do with the time spent together. Conversely he also is entitled not to have others express any expectations or objections on this score."[7]

Nevertheless, no matter how hard they try, arrogant, vindictive people can never completely eliminate their needs for warmth, compassion and acceptance. No matter how much their iron self-expectations deny it, even they also like approval.

In contrast to this need, however, Horney describes the dominating fear of vindictive triumph as "getting too soft." Because genuine affection has typically been lacking in their childhoods, these individuals have convinced themselves, in order to survive, that they do not need affection anyway. Early experiences with neglect, humiliation and a lack of sympathy have promoted a hardness toward life and other people. A pervasive distrust in human closeness blinds them to their genuine need for noncompetitive human contact:

> He gradually "decides" that genuine affection is not only unattainable for him but that it does not exist at all. He ends up by no longer wanting it and even rather scorning it. This, however, is a step of grave consequence, because the need for affection, for human warmth and closeness is a powerful incentive for developing qualities that make us likeable. The feeling of being loved and—even more—of being lovable is perhaps one of the greatest values in life.[8]

Thus, this unconscious suspicion of unlovability pushes arrogant-vindictives to eliminate any softness in life, to deny their own desperate longing for unconditional love, and to continue a vicious form of competition. They do not relate to others; they dominate them. They do not share with others; they conquer them.

These, then, are the three major ways people move against others in the self-expansive solution: narcissism, perfectionism and vindictive triumph. It

---

[7] Ibid., p. 200.
[8] Ibid., p. 202.

is important to emphasize the extent to which all three expressions of the self-mastery solution insist on a conscious control of the world. This pride insists on a denial of unconscious processes. To admit the influence of the unconscious is to open a door of fear. Self-mastery persons must be the masters of their fate! Any talk of unconscious activity must be scoffed at or denied.[9] Perhaps more than anything else, the realm of the unconscious threatens the mastery with which they take charge of their world.

Clearly, pride, rather than low self-esteem, seems to be dominant in this self-expansive solution. Horney's emphasis seems to match the Augustinian tradition's diagnosis of the exalted self. However, as we shall later see, this pride may be built on a fragile foundation that includes self-contempt.

2. Moving toward others: the self-effacing solution. Moving toward people involves an attempt to accommodate them, win their affection or approval and reduce any possibility of conflict. The primary ingredient here is compliance. This produces a feeling of safety. Goodness, love and saintliness are often the driving images in this solution. Any form of self-assertion, pride, ambition or initiative is consciously prohibited. One must never, under any circumstance, feel superior to anyone. "In sharp contrast to the expansive types, he lives with a diffuse failure (to measure up to his shoulds) and hence tends to feel guilty, inferior, or contemptible."[10] Thus, a radical taboo on any form of pride is combined with a fear of self-expansion. Anything associated with ambition, vindictiveness, triumph or getting ahead is considered anathema. "If we realize in detail the scope covered by the taboos, they constitute a crippling check on the person's expansion, his capacity for fighting and for defending himself, his self-interest—on anything that might accrue to his growth or his self-esteem. The taboos and self-minimizing constitute a *shrinking process.*"[11]

Horney points out that even winning at various games may threaten the need to be a subdued self. Asserting basic rights provokes guilt over any possibility of intruding on others. Apologies drop constantly from the mouth of self-effacing persons:

---

[9]Ibid., p. 192.
[10]Ibid., p. 215.
[11]Ibid., p. 219 (italics in original).

Even when making perfectly legitimate requests he feels as though he
were taking undue advantage of the other person. And he either re-
frains from asking or does it apologetically, with a "guilty" conscience.
He may even be helpless toward people who are actually dependent
upon him, and cannot defend himself when they treat him in an in-
sulting fashion. No wonder then that he is an easy prey for people
who are out to take advantage of him. He is defenseless, often becomes aware of it only much later, and may then react with intense
anger at himself and the exploiter.[12]

Any form of self-assertion, such as speaking up for legitimate rights, is
perceived as selfish, rude and aggressive. If one wants anything beyond what
he or she has, it is condemned as a lack of gratitude. All things done for oneself are selfish. In fact, any experience enjoyed alone is selfish.[13]

Self-effacing persons have enormous difficulty giving themselves credit
for any accomplishment. The chronic fear is "being presumptuous." They
must live within the narrow confines of a humble world. Genuine accomplishments are always reduced to "lucky breaks."

In addition, the thought of conflict, and particularly anyone being hostile
toward them, triggers an automatic tendency to give in, "forgive" and take
a subordinate position. They are allowed to dislike no one. Hostility cannot
be sustained, even though unconsciously it is deeply felt. Grudges are simply not permitted.

Many times self-effacing persons will minimize another's criticism of
them by an eagerness to admit inadequacy or take responsibility for things
outside their control. By pointing out their own faults in advance, they take
the sting out of possible criticism. By being constantly apologetic, they attempt to elicit sympathetic assurance.[14] It's as if they are saying, "I'll criticize
myself before you have a chance to."

This "peace at all costs" interpersonal philosophy is more understandable
when we realize that for the self-effacing person, "salvation lies in others."[15]

---

[12]Ibid., pp. 216-17.
[13]Ibid., p. 218.
[14]Ibid. p. 219.
[15]Ibid., p. 226.

In other words, others are essential to escape their inner world of self-contempt. Constant attempts to please others serve as a temporary fix from the world of feeling inadequate. Self-effacing persons cannot afford to be discriminating about other people. They crave everyone's approval. Horney points out the compulsive quality in the self-effacing person's need for acceptance:

> On the surface it looks as though he had an unshakable faith in the essential goodness of humanity. And it is true that he is more open, more sensitive, to likable qualities in others. But the compulsiveness of his expectations makes it impossible for him to be discriminating. He cannot as a rule distinguish between genuine friendliness and its many counterfeits. He is too easily bribed by any show of warmth or interest. In addition, his inner dictates tell him that he *should* like everybody, that he *should* not be suspicious. Finally, his fear of antagonism and possible fights makes him overlook, discard, minimize, or explain away such traits as lying, crookedness, exploiting, cruelty, treachery.[16]

Horney goes on to say that even when they are confronted with the exploitation, deceit and manipulation of others, the self-effacing person tends to believe that they really didn't mean it. Realizing the destructive intent of others is practically impossible. Why? The answer lies in the exaggerated role others play. To actually believe that others are capable of malevolence undermines their own method of psychological redemption, since that redemption is always in the hands of others. Stated differently, if acceptance is desperately needed from others, the discovery that these others may not have the capacity to offer it disturbs their solution to the anxiety problem. They have a vested interest in seeing everyone as essentially good. Admitting the malevolence of others threatens to cut off their much needed supply of approval.

But what, exactly, are these individuals' salvific needs? Horney describes them as an excessive need for affection, love, sympathy and approval. This solution to the anxiety problem insists that love is the answer to everything, so they dare not risk its loss, even at the price of their own integrity. Thus,

---

[16]Ibid.

they must automatically live up to others' standards. Horney very poign-
antly describes this condition as having their "center of gravity" in others
rather than within themselves.[17] They are controlled by their dread of self-
assertion and their fear of hostility, both in themselves and in others.[18]

Part of this self-effacing solution also involves the need for a partner who
will take over their lives and fulfill all of these expectations for love, belong-
ing, approval and so on. This places a premium on "love" because love will
solve all problems.[19] Any possibility of abandonment creates enormous anxiety as the thought of being alone is nearly unbearable. Horney character-
izes a woman who practically sells her soul to accommodate a partner:

> The first characteristic to strike us is such a woman's total absorption in
> the relationship. The partner becomes the sole center of her existence.
> Everything revolves around him. Her mood depends upon whether his
> attitude toward her is more positive or negative. She does not dare make
> any plans lest she might miss a call or an evening with him. Her endeav-
> ors are directed toward measuring up to what she feels he expects. She
> has but one fear—that of antagonizing and losing him. Conversely her
> other interests subside. Her work, unless connected with him, becomes
> comparatively meaningless. This may even be true of professional work
> otherwise dear to her heart, or productive work in which she has ac-
> complished things. Naturally the latter suffers most.[20]

Note that the above description was written in 1950, nearly three decades
before American culture became fascinated with the phenomenon of codependency.

In order to insure that the "partner" (who is actually not a partner at all)
does not leave, self-effacing persons must restrict their lives within very narrow borders. They must be content with very little and essentially stifle all
their ambitions. Any wish for material things is perceived as selfish. There is
a strong need to "remain inconspicuous and to take second place."[21] Mod-

---

[17]Karen Horney, *Self-Analysis* (New York: W. W. Norton, 1942), p. 51.
[18]Ibid.
[19]Ibid., p. 52.
[20]Karen Horney, *Neurosis and Human Growth* (New York: W. W. Norton, 1950), pp. 247-48.
[21]Horney, *Self-Analysis*, p. 52.

esty is the supreme value and any hint of arrogance must be quickly crushed. Unconsciously, of course, they are proud of their lack of pride.

It is not uncommon for self-effacing persons to marry self-expansive types. One of the primary reasons for this, according to Horney, is that while self-mastery is forbidden within self-effacing persons, they admire it in others. Horney believes that, unconsciously, self-effacing persons envy self-assertive and even aggressive behavior in others. Disavowing any possibility of self-assurance within themselves, they secretly admire steel self-confidence in others. In fact, they may externalize their own need for self-mastery and vicariously experience it through another. They won't allow it to emerge within themselves, but they are free to enjoy it in others.

Horney also suggests that self-abnegating people gravitate toward self-expansive types because any sign of "weakness" in another serves as a mirror of their own weakness.[22] The idea of having to be the stronger one in a relationship is petrifying. Consequently, they lean toward those who seem to have a mastery of life. In fact, they may even have a fascination with arrogance and aggressiveness in others, since these traits are so severely repressed within their own psyches.

These needs of the self-effacing individual quickly become claims to which he or she feels entitled: "'I am entitled to love, affection, understanding, sympathy. I am entitled to have things done for me. I am entitled not to the pursuit of happiness but to have happiness fall into my lap.' It goes almost without saying that these claims—as claims—remain more unconscious than in the expansive solution."[23] The urgency with which these needs are craved leads quickly to demands that they be met. Consciously, of course, it would be much too selfish to admit these demands that they place on others. Yet beneath conscious awareness these expectations insist on being met.

The self-effacing solution may, on the surface, look like inordinate low self-esteem and a highly self-depreciating attitude. Yet below this layer is an unconscious pride system that insists that they "not be like others." After all,

---

[22]Horney, *Neurosis and Human Growth*, p. 244.
[23]Ibid., pp. 228-29.

they have "higher" standards. A rather grandiose image of radical selflessness and perfect self-sacrifice operates behind stage. It is precisely the *pride* behind their self-effacing attitude that often makes it hard to give up. Put another way, they are getting unconscious mileage out of it. The demanding selfless image insists that they eradicate self-concern, yet their unconscious need to maintain this image promotes self-concern. They are afraid of their pride, yet they run away from it in the name of a higher form of pride.

This analysis seems to side with Niebuhr's conviction that even self-abnegating behavior is ultimately based on a form of pride. It may be fruitless to address behavioral changes with self-effacing persons until they see the inner dictates that drive their guilt and self-belittling behavior. Beneath self-contempt lurks grandiosity.

Obviously, no one can successfully live up to the pride system of the self-effacing position. Yet the proud element in this solution is precisely the conviction that they can. The underlying belief in the possibility of their perfect self-abnegation reveals an unconscious self-exaltation. Furthermore, regardless of how self-depreciating they are, they will, at least at an unconscious level, resent interpersonal injustices, want particular things and desire some degree of power and status. They may consciously will these things away, but they exist underground.

Clearly, these self-effacing persons are the ones feminist have in mind when they critique Niebuhr's excessive emphasis on pride. Self-effacing persons need to be more self-assertive, so how can pride be their problem? Horney's insistence that self-abnegation also has an underside of pride is in agreement with Niebuhr. In a sense, she offers support to both views, but as we will continue to see, she believes it is quite impossible to separate pride and self-contempt.

3. Moving away from others: the self-resignation solution. The movement away from others attempts to resolve anxiety through detachment or aloofness. The "solution" in this movement is evasion. All interpersonal relationships are perceived as sticky, and one is far better off to be isolated and build a world unto oneself. Wisdom, self-sufficiency and independence are the cardinal virtues here. What must be avoided is the feeling of needing anyone or being close to them. Being close brings up engulfment fears. Relationships, it is believed, tend to involve hostages. Distance and separateness are the only source of security.[24] To guarantee peace, it is necessary to leave the battleground of interpersonal relationships, where there is a constant threat of being captured. Resigned persons must convince themselves that they simply don't care: "Where the compliant type looks at his fellow man with the silent question, 'Will he like me'—and the aggressive type wants to know, 'How strong an adversary is he?' or 'Can he be useful to me?'—the detached person's first concern is, 'Will he interfere with me. Will he want to influence me or will he leave me alone?'"[25]

Horney distinguishes between constructive and compulsive resignation. Constructive resignation simply realizes the futility of many ambitions and drives for success. This is the wisdom of older persons who have mellowed their expectations of life and cease to be demanding about what life owes them. The rat race is not worth it. This attitude often involves a renunciation of nonessentials in life so that we can focus on ultimate matters.[26] It is a healthy detachment.

Compulsive resignation as a "solution" to the problem of anxiety, however, is quite different. It simply wants an absence of conflict. "His resignation, therefore is a process of shrinking, of restricting, of curtailing life and growth."[27] The desire for life without pain or friction also means a life without zest.[28] Escaping all forms of obligation or duty, the motto of resigned persons is "we don't want to be bothered." In a sense, resigned persons are spectators of their own lives.

Another prime characteristic of this self-resigning tendency is the elimination of any form of ambition. This is often accompanied by a hatred of any expenditure of effort. Horney further suggests that these individuals are masters at finding reasons for *not* doing things. Goal-directed activity or planning is treated with suspicion. It is a bother. The essence of prohibition is a "restriction of wishes."[29] Self-resigning persons believe they should not wish for or expect anything. The secret of happiness is to not desire very much. "The two outstanding neurotic claims are that life should be easy,

---

[24]Horney, *Self-Analysis,* p. 55.

[25]Horney, *Our Inner Conflicts,* p. 80.

[26]Horney, *Neurosis and Human Growth,* pp. 259-60.

[27]Ibid., p. 260.

[28]Ibid.

[29]Ibid., p. 263.

painless, and effortless and that he should not be bothered."[30]

A constant underlying fear of self-resigned persons is getting so attached to someone that we need them. There should be no one we "can't do without." Transitory relationships often guarantee that we will not become dependent and will remain safe in our detachment. Resigned persons always look for the exit signs when they enter the room.

Resigned persons are also hypersensitive to pressure, coercion or influence.[31] They constantly fear being "taken over" by someone else's wishes. The desires of others could easily impair their freedom. An intense worry about being dominated continually fuels the detachment. Horney offers a nice summary of this position: "He feels entitled to having others not intrude upon his privacy, to having them not expect anything of him or bother him, to be exempt from having to make a living and from responsibilities.[32] Anxiety-reduction is thus linked to distance from others. Out of fear of being absorbed, controlled, invaded or crowded, the resignation solution forfeits human closeness.

COMMON BONDS IN ALL THREE MOVEMENTS

While each of these anxiety-reducing movements may appear quite different, they have in common some specific themes. First, they all block the possibility of genuine intimacy with another. They each forbid the potential of an equal-regard relationship. The moving-against, self-expansive person, out of anxiety and fear of equality, must dominate, conquer and control. The narcissistic form of this movement needs a constant audience, not an equal partner; the perfectionist form will invariably set up a parent-child, condescending attitude because of "high standards"; and the hypercompetitive form simply must dominate in order to feel in control.

Similarly, moving-toward, compliant persons are too "needy" to share a mutually strong relationship. They, too, know nothing of win-win solutions because their denial of their own genuine wants, preferences and goals defaults the possibility of meeting another person halfway. Instead, a massive accommodation attempts to sooth their anxiety.

---

[30]Ibid., p. 264.
[31]Ibid., p. 266.
[32]Ibid., p. 271.

And finally, the resignation solution has so many engulfment fears that it forever regards intimacy as suspicious, as always containing a trap behind the closeness. So all three movements curtail genuine intimacy.

Another factor in all three solutions is the inevitability of egocentricity. This egocentricity separates the neurotic from others. But Horney points out that egocentricity means far more than selfishness or self-adoration:

> By egocentricity I do not mean selfishness or egotism in the sense of considering merely one's own advantage. The neurotic may be callously selfish or too unselfish—there is nothing in this regard that is characteristic for all neuroses. But he is always egocentric in the sense of being wrapped up in himself. This need not be apparent on the surface—he may be a lone wolf or live for and through others. Nevertheless he lives in any case by his private religion (his idealized image), abides by his own laws (his shoulds), within the barbed-wire fence of his own pride and with his guards to protect him against dangers from within and without. As a result he not only becomes more isolated emotionally but it also becomes more difficult for him to see other people as individuals in their own right, different from himself. They are subordinated to his prime concern: himself.[33]

It is very difficult to address others in their own right when we can't get outside the prison of our needs. We may need them to admire us, to buckle under us, to always be wrong, to take over our lives or to leave us alone. We also need them in order to escape our own self-hatred. What would we do without someone to project upon? Simply stated, we always need others to be something *for us.* This burden laid on others does not allow them to be who they are, and hence, it contaminates relationships.

Another common denominator in these three movements, according to Horney, is the unconscious sense of being unlovable.[34] We may feel that others love our looks, our intelligence, our status and power or other particular traits. However, beneath this surface lurks a deep-seated conviction that our essence is somehow unlovable.

---

[33]Ibid., pp. 291-92.
[34]Ibid., pp. 299-300.

Horney identifies three reasons for this feeling of unlovableness.[35] First, we may believe we are unlovable because our own ability to love others is impaired. We may be so wrapped up with our own needs that it becomes very difficult to be attentive to others. We can't be available to others because we can't get out of the death-grip of our own insecurity and need to prove something. Conversely, if our capacity to love is developed, we will not spend so much time worrying about whether or not we are loveable. A second contributing factor to the sense of unlovability is the extent of our self-hate and its necessary externalization. As long as self-hate governs our attitude toward ourselves, it is quite difficult to believe anyone else could really love us.[36] A third factor is our expecting more of love than love can possibly ever give. Consequently, we are constantly dissatisfied. When love does not deliver our unrealistic demands, we assume we must be unlovable. The problem, of course, is in our exalted view of what love will do for us.

While each person has the capacity for all three of these unhealthy movements, one will typically dominate. This pattern, starting in childhood, often carries into adulthood. New experiences will be understood or interpreted through the framework of one of these dominant patterns. An aggressive person will think another's friendliness is stupid or an attempt to manipulate. A detached person will think another person's friendliness contains all sorts of hidden demands that threaten autonomy. As a result, this interpretation reinforces the particular pattern for handling anxiety.

As we have seen, these patterns are compulsively driven. The "solution" may be completely inappropriate for the situation, yet we simply "must" act in this rigid way. A person may occasionally shift patterns (going, let's say, from self-effacing to self-isolating), but this is not often, and the new pattern will be organized around the rigid needs of that particular trend. We become bound to a rigid pattern. Yet none of them provide the security we crave. Put theologically, none of the moves are salvific. They do not save us from the human dilemma, the problem of our precarious nature. Put in Niebuhrian terms, they do not relieve us from the tensions of being a juxtaposition of nature and spirit. Anxiety is inevitable and inescapable.

---

[35]Ibid.
[36]Ibid., p. 300.

In spite of their doomed nature, each of these solutions offers the promise of psychological redemption because it contains an image of the perfect
self that keeps pushing us along. This concept of the idealized self is clearly
one of Horney's most valuable contributions. It is indispensable for understanding our conflict between pride and self-contempt.

THE IDEALIZED SELF

Throughout the development of her work, Horney shifted from an emphasis on the interpersonal causes of anxiety to a greater emphasis on anxiety's
intrapsychic roots. Put differently, she began to view anxiety more as a
problem in our relationship to ourselves. Granted, as we have seen, we develop early "solutions" to our problem of relating to others as we tend to
move toward, against or away form them. However, that hardly ends the
anxiety discussion. Neurosis does not emerge simply in our relationships
with others but also in relationship to ourselves. As we shall see, in this shift
to intrapsychic anxiety, Horney moves closer to the position of Niebuhr. In
fact, she makes some interesting comments about the relationship of anxiety
to finitude, which sound as if they fell directly from the mouth of Niebuhr.
Bernard Paris provides a good summary of Horney's shift:

> In *Neurosis and Human Growth* Horney posits a developmental se-
> quence that leads from interpersonal to intrapsychic strategies of de-
> fense. Children try to cope with feelings of weakness, inadequacy, and
> isolation by developing interpersonal strategies. They then must deal
> with the conflicts between these strategies by making one of them
> predominant and suppressing the others. The coherence thus achieved
> is too loose, and the children need a firmer and more comprehensive
> *integration.* The original defenses, moreover, do not fully satisfy their
> psychological needs and exacerbate their sense of weakness by alien-
> ating children from their real selves. As a further defense children or
> adolescents develop an idealized image of themselves, which is a kind
> of artistic creation in which opposites appear reconciled.[37]

---

[37]Bernard Paris, *Karen Horney: A Psychoanalyst's Search for Self-Understanding* (New Haven, Conn.: Yale
University Press, 1994), p. 201.

This idealized self, to which Paris refers, is an image of what we should be, must be or ought to be, in order to be acceptable. The idealized self-image is born out of the imagination and is quite impossible to actualize. It is a romanticized portrait built on exaggerated self-expectations. The idealized self stands above the traffic of everyday reality, exalted and endowed with what seems like unlimited power and significance. It attempts to find a solution to the conflicts of life by escaping through the imagination.

Trying to live within the idealized self's restrictive, rigid conception of life always involves enormous denial. We begin to avoid aspects of our own experience that do not conform to our elevated image of ideal personhood. Horney refers to this as self-alienation, which means roughly the same thing as Rogerian incongruence. We gradually become a stranger to ourselves. The actual self, consisting of our real feelings and experience, becomes twisted, distorted and stretched into a mold of the "appropriate" self. This censorship activity has the end result of self-estrangement and ignorance of our real needs, desires and dispositions toward life. The neurotic trick, of course, is to somehow to maintain the pseudo-image. We must falsify reality and discard all disturbing evidence to the contrary:

> Roughly speaking, a person builds up an idealized image of himself because he cannot tolerate himself as he actually is. The image apparently counteracts this calamity; but having placed himself on a pedestal, he can tolerate his real self still less and starts to rage against it, to despise himself and to chafe under the yoke of his own unattainable demands upon himself. He wavers then between self-adoration and self-contempt, between his idealized image and his despised image, with no solid middle ground to fall back on.[38]

The specific features of the idealized self vary from person to person, depending on the particular structure of the personality. For some, power may be the dominant factor. For others, beauty, intelligence, saintliness or patience may be the governing factors in the creation of the idealized self. The extent to which the idealized image is unrealistic determines the level of arrogance necessary. Interestingly, Horney points out that the word *arrogance*

---

[38]Horney, *Our Inner Conflicts,* p. 112.

comes from *arrogate,* which means to attribute to ourselves qualities that we do not have. These traits may be potentialities, but they are not actualities. So obviously, the more extravagant the idealized self, the more we must arrogate pretentious qualities.

The overwhelming amount of psychic energy necessary to maintain an inflated self depletes the energy needed to achieve our actual potential. The more exaggerated the self-claims, the more likely the outside evidence discounts the idealized image. Thus, an intrapsychic scrambling process is necessarily involved in maintaining this pseudo-self. As Horney points out, we do not need much confirmation for qualities about which we feel sure. But false claims about ourselves do leave us feeling defensive and touchy.

The particular content of the idealized self will be largely shaped by the dominating neurotic solution established in childhood. For instance, if we have elected the self-effacing, moving-toward-others solution, the idealized self will revolve around "lovable qualities" such as selflessness, generosity, compassion, goodness or saintliness. This solution will glorify "helplessness, suffering, and martyrdom."[39] Conversely, any thought of self-expression or self-concern will be judged as a kind of selfish blasphemy against the dictates of the idealized self, which must be "perfectly self-giving."

If, on the other hand, we move against others in arrogant, vindictive ways, the idealized self will pivot around images of being smarter, tougher, stronger and more in control than others. Any hint of weakness will be deemed anathema. We must be the master of our situation! Whether this tendency involves obvious narcissism, perfectionism or a compulsive drive toward vindictive triumph, the constant theme is self-mastery and control.

Finally, if we move away from others in isolation and detachment, the idealized self will possess complete self-sufficiency, autonomous serenity, the freedom from being bothered by interpersonal confusions, and a disengaged, stoical sense of peace. The idea of complete freedom from all pressure will be magnified as the salvific agent for the psyche.

The idealized self always propels one of these images, pushing like a slave-driver for the particular solution. The idealized self in the compliance approach is free of conflict; in the aggressive approach, free of weakness; and

---

[39] Horney, *Neurosis and Human Growth,* p. 222.

in the isolated approach, free of dependency on others. In all these solutions, *pride governs feelings*.[40] The "pride system," which we will later discuss in more detail, allows only those feelings that lie within the parameters of the idealized self. It operates on the principle that Horney often calls the "supremacy of the mind." Feelings are frequently unruly and therefore need to be treated as suspicious invaders in the psychic world. They must be "brought in line" with the idealized self. This is accomplished through the mind—the imagination and reason. The self-expansive person must never experience feelings of helplessness; the self-abnegating person must never experience feelings of pride; and the self-resigning person must never experience feelings of dependency. In each case, a stern idealized self will not allow these feelings to persist.

The creation and maintenance of the idealized self is primarily an unconscious maneuver. Riddled with a hounding sense of self-dissatisfaction and contempt, the psyche produces a simple survival scheme: If I am unsatisfied with my actual self, why not retreat into the lab of denial and create an ideal self? Why settle on who I really am? Instead, I can grant my imagination power to manufacture a suitable, though illusory, image. I can then twist my experience so that it matches the portrait I want. Again, it is precisely this process, carried out with intricate subtlety, that keeps us from experiencing our genuine self and robs us of the energies we need to pursue realistic potentials. Put more theologically, as long as we are chasing our idealized self and ignoring the realities of who we really are, we cancel the possibilities of the transforming power of "grace in the gut," that is, the kind of ontological acceptance that prizes us for the limited human beings we are. As long as the imagination controls how we perceive ourselves, the actual self is off-limits. And when the actual self is off-limits, grace cannot be received in the depths of our being. Instead, we desperately try to earn this acceptance. Horney, in what is perhaps her most vivid statement about the idealized self, describes the person caught in its grip:

> He should be the utmost of honesty, generosity, considerateness, justice, dignity, courage, unselfishness. He should be the perfect lover,

---

[40]Ibid., p. 162.

husband, teacher. He should be able to endure everything, should like everybody, should love his parents, his wife, his country; or, he should not be attached to anything or anybody, nothing should matter to him, he should never feel hurt, and he should always be serene and unruffled. He should always enjoy life; or, he should be above pleasure and enjoyment. He should be spontaneous; he should always control his feelings. He should know, understand, and foresee everything. He should be able to solve every problem of his own, or of others, in no time. He should be able to overcome every difficulty of his as soon as he sees it. He should never be tired or fall ill. He should always be able to find a job. He should be able to do things in one hour which can only be done in two to three hours.[41]

Horney frequently uses images from literature to provide examples of her insightful comments. A helpful image to describe the idealized self comes from Mary Shelly's famous novel *Frankenstein*.[42] The idealized self is in many ways like Dr. Frankenstein's monster. Initially, this creation seemed to be a marvelous production. Yet the monster ended up turning against the creative doctor, ultimately destroying him. Similarly, the idealized self is a created monster who turns on and seeks to destroy the actual self.

Another powerful example of this internal war between the idealized self and the actual self is Robert Louis Stevenson's classic tale *Dr. Jekyll and Mr. Hyde*.[43] The upright Victorian physician Henry Jekyll wanted desperately to embody fully his idealized self. In an effort to get rid of those annoying aspects of his personality that did not match this idealized portrait, he created a potion. His treatment of the actual self had been harsh, pretentious and highly self-righteous. On the other side of his chemical concoction, he did not find a blissful state of faultlessness. On the contrary, his repressed side lunged forth with a hunger for life and a rebellious knack for pointing out Jekyll's phoniness. Indeed, Mr. Hyde also hated Dr. Jekyll and all his Victorian expectations for a perfectly ordered life. Horney depicts this process: "The actual, empirical self becomes the offensive stranger to whom the ide-

---

[41]Ibid., p. 65.
[42]Ibid., p. 118.
[43]Ibid., pp. 189-90.

alized self happens to be tied, and the latter turns against this stranger with hate and contempt. The actual self becomes the victim of the proud idealized self."[44] Thus, Horney describes this condition as not just a split, but a cruel and murderous battle. She says, "We must realize the rage of the proud self for feeling humiliated and held down at every step by the actual self."[45] Jekyll hated the appalling antics of Mr. Hyde, and Hyde, in turn, detested the hypocrisy of the good doctor. The severity of this inner war ended in self-destruction. Jekyll, the idealized self, could never "own" Mr. Hyde as part of his own being. The split destroyed him.

The creation of the idealized self is not simply a one-time act. Instead, it is a continual creation. The image must be fueled, and this demands much attention to its unrealistic standards that deny reality. Put simply, it's an ongoing, full-time job that absorbs the energies that could have been used for the service of self-realization, or what Rogers calls self-actualization.

THREE RESPONSES TO THE IDEALIZED SELF

The idealized self frequently has an authoritarian, dictatorial nature. This tends to provoke three responses. The first is to completely identify with the superior image. When we do this, argues Horney, we are not conscious of the rift between the idealized and actual self. We believe we are as perfect as our portrait. We are the inflated narcissists. We consciously believe in their exalted self.

The second response is to try desperately to measure up. Constantly trying, enduring and believing that one day we can "get it right," we are perfectionists. We are always "on our way."

The third response is either chronic self-berating and self-contempt or the projection of that self-contempt onto others. Here a low self-esteem seems most obvious. In this third response it is harder to see the pride system that may be operating behind the low self-esteem.

Much of the time we think the demands of the idealized self somehow exist outside of us. In fact, we may rebel against those unrealistic expectations, not recognizing that the demands arise from within ourselves. Exter-

---

[44] Ibid., p. 112.
[45] Ibid., p. 114.

nalizing self-contempt is far easier than experiencing it from ourselves. The pain of recognizing our own self-contempt would be too much:

> To feel all his own scorn would smash whatever spurious self-assurance the neurotic may have and bring him to the verge of collapse. It is painful enough to be despised by others, but there is always hope of being able to change their attitude, or a prospect of paying them back in kind. When it is oneself one despises, all this is of no avail. There is no court of appeal. All the hopelessness the neurotic unconsciously feels in regard to himself would come into clear relief.[46]

In reality, the internal pressure of the idealized self is much worse than any external pressure. Thus, we use "other people" to diffuse the self-hatred. Condemned by the demands of the idealized self, we assume that others hold us in as much contempt as we hold ourselves. A merciless attitude toward self is therefore pushed off onto others. Mistakes will be met with compassionless condemnation. Others will have zero tolerance for our errors.

PRIDE AND SELF-HATE

A central theme in Horney's work deals with the prevalence of self-hate. Though often repressed, it is always the flip side of pride. It is this discussion of the relationship between pride and self-contempt that offers the greatest promise for resolving our debate between the overvalued self (Niebuhr) and the undervalued self (Rogers). Horney believes we may become aware of our self-hate during stressful moments, but then we often forget about it. Yet it is still very much active at an unconscious level. We may say that we merely have temporary feelings of being stupid, for instance, but those feelings often pulsate with intensity in the unconscious. According to Horney, even people who are aware of their self-recriminations often have no idea how destructive the process actually is.

It is far easier to notice the results or consequences of self-hate than to recognize it as the cause of those consequences. For instance, feeling chronically guilty, inferior, cramped or inwardly tormented may actually be the direct consequence of self-contempt. As we have noted, it is frequently too

---

[46]Horney, *Our Inner Conflicts*, p. 119.

painful to experience the direct fury of self-hate, so it must be externalized, our feelings shifted to an outsider. Externalization can be active or passive. Active externalization involves a hatred of other people, institutions or even the entire outside world. Severe cynicism about outside factors is necessary to avoid the inner disgust with our own being. Conversely, passive externalization involves believing that the outside world hates us. Rather than facing our own self-contempt, we transfer it to the outside world. The external world is against us, hostile and antagonistic. We may even call our paranoia worldly wisdom. The point is that we shift the persecution from an intrapsychic source to an outside source.

One of the most insightful contributions Horney has offered is the distinction between neurotic self-accusations and a healthy conscience. The pivotal point is that excessive guilt always emerges from neurotic pride. The dictates of the idealized self mercilessly judge the inevitable problems of being human, with no regard whatsoever for the actual self. Excessive guilt expresses the discontent of the proud self with the actual self. We have not met the standards of the unrealistic requirements. Often, the actual self cowers in the unconscious, afraid of the punishments from the internal dictator.

A healthy conscience, on the other hand, guards the best interest of the true self as it calls us back to our realistic values and standards. The purpose of guilt here is education, not humiliation. It is a reminder that we are acting inconsistently with our own standards. Maybe those standards need to be reexamined. We need not feel crushed by the awareness of our own shortcomings and human frailty. Unlike the demands of the idealized self, a healthy conscience does not beat us with shame: "our conscience is a moral agency serving our growth, while self-accusations are amoral in origin and immoral in effect because they keep the individual from soberly examining his existing difficulties and thereby interfere with his human growth."[47]

Horney believes we can witness four consequences of self-hatred. One is a compulsive need to compare self with others. Typically, the result is a "comparative inferiority." The other person is always smarter, better looking, more professional, better informed and so on. This relentless comparison of self with others is necessary because we have already made an

---

[47]Horney, *Neurosis and Human Growth*, p. 131.

unconscious claim of superiority. We "should" be superior. The self-berating we experience in comparison is only possible because we are supposed to be better than everyone else. This dynamic reveals the subtle relationship of pride and self-contempt. In this sense, low self-esteem is an outgrowth of pride. Basic anxiety has pushed us toward ditching the real self and making unconscious claims of superiority. This fragile sense of superiority constantly flies in the face of evidence to the contrary. This evidence then provokes a comparative inferiority and castigating self-criticism. We feel beaten down with a sense of inadequacy. Yet the severity of the inadequacy depends entirely on the pride system's demand that we must be superior to all others. Thus, we often set ourselves up for self-loathing because of the arrogance of our self-expectations. Pride and self-contempt alternate between foreground and background on our psychological canvass.

Another consequence of self-hate is a hypersensitivity to criticism, and hence, an excessive vulnerability in our relationships. As we have seen, if we hate ourselves, it is easy to assume others hate us. Our hypersensitivity to the idealized self's criticism makes it essential to believe others are unfairly critical, not us. We dare not turn those negative guns on ourselves. None of us can live with chronic, conscious self-contempt. Therefore we have a vested interest in regarding others as the real critics and offenders.[48]

Still another consequence of self-hate is allowing too much abuse from others.[49] We can hardly estimate the horrendous effects on self-esteem when we allow others to physically, emotionally, financially or spiritually abuse us. As scores of women in domestic violence situations can attest, getting out is often easier said than done. Threats on our life and the lives of our children, questions about a place to live, food for our kids and other matters are very real. However, the acceptance of abuse, as has been so frequently pointed out, often leads us to believe that we deserve nothing better. Self-esteem has been whittled down to the point that we do not consider ourselves worthy of standing as an equal. The abuse demoralizes and tears away the last strands of self-respect.

This extremely negative impact of abuse on self-esteem must be clearly

---

[48]Ibid., p. 136.
[49]Ibid.

recognized. However, that is not always the whole story. I make this point with great hesitation for fear of being misunderstood and seeming insensitive to persons who are suffering. Yet pride can also be mixed in with the tolerance of too much abuse. Beneath what appears to be a crushed level of self-esteem, the pride system is often operative. But how? Doesn't this sound like the very worst form of blaming the victim?

Some persons allow abuse because their idealized self is demanding that they be the epitome of patience, tolerance, forgiveness and long-suffering. Recognizing their rights, expecting equality, insisting on interpersonal compromise are all prohibited by an idealized self who has made a god out of "not complaining." "Always be appreciative of what you have," "never gripe about anything" and "find something good in everyone" are often the dictates of neurotic pride that keep a person bound to a destructive situation. When we encounter these individuals, we often see only the self-contempt side of their passivity. But it is necessary to help some abused persons see the driving, unrealistic expectations that often come from their pride. They are arrogating to themselves qualities that they "should" have, yet are ones not humanly possible. Other people get angry, but they are not supposed to; other people demand fairness, but their idealized self would never allow that; other people get out of unhealthy situations, but they never give up on anybody.

Many who work with these individuals make noble attempts to help them construct higher self-esteem. I would like to suggest, however, that this work needs to be complemented by helping them deconstruct their pride system. Simply telling them they are "too hard on themselves" will not do. Instead, it is important to help them see the inflated nature of their idealized self and how it has served to keep them from knowing the real self. Thus, even in cases that seem to involve enormous layers of self-contempt, it is important to remember that a low self-esteem problem is also a pride problem.

Another example is the individual who almost constantly feels stupid or unintelligent. What appears to be the obvious need here is to help build up that person's intellectual confidence. The issue, once again, is low self-esteem, pure and simple, right? Not exactly. Instead, we have another example of pride intermingled with the obvious low self-esteem problem. Beneath the negative view of one's "stupidity," there is often a pride system that expects omniscience. Again, it is precisely because we have inflated our sense of intellectual capacity that we live with such derogatory self-evaluations: "The self-disparaging concerning intelligence, with the resultant feeling of stupidity, corresponds to pride in the omnipotence of reason. And it depends upon the whole structure as to whether pride or self-contempt on this score is in the foreground. . . . The compelling need to appear omniscient may interfere with the capacity to learn."[50]

The last consequence of self-hate is the compulsive need to alleviate self-contempt with attention, regard, appreciation or admiration from others. These persons often seem insatiable. They wear us out. Sometimes after being around them, we may not be sure why we feel so drained. Often we feel frustrated as we realize the interaction with them is never mutual, but always one way—namely, we give them our time, attention and energy. Yet there is a pitiful cry in their constant effort to perform for us. Clearly, they go from person to person trying to get something they need.

Perhaps what is overlooked in this "obvious" form of low self-esteem is the underlying pride system that says that everyone *ought* to like me or that I am completely loveable. The constant attempt to win approval and affection is based on a conviction that we can win those things from everyone. There is a double grandiosity here: (1) that we can control what others think of us and (2) that everyone will like us if we simply work at it. Thus, even here, pride and low self-esteem appear to be mixed together.

THE "SEARCH FOR GLORY"

"What exactly does the neurotic despise in himself?" Horney asks. She answers: "Sometimes everything: his human limitations; his body, its appearance and functioning; the faculties of his mind—reasoning, memory, critical thinking, planning, special skills or gifts—any activity from simple private actions to public performances."[51]

The extent of this self-hate, either consciously or unconsciously, sets us on a "search for glory," another of Horney's concepts that sounds quite Niebuhrian. This search for glory always entails an attempt to reach beyond

---

[50]Ibid., p. 139.
[51]Ibid., p. 137.

what is humanly possible. "All the drives for glory have in common the reaching out for greater knowledge, wisdom, virtue, or powers than are given to human beings; they all aim at the *absolute,* the unlimited, the infinite."[52] The similarity with Niebuhr's understanding of pride is unmistakable. Our refusal to accept our finitude provokes in us a restless attempt to attain a godlike status. Yet also note Horney's similarity with Rogers. The search for glory is a distortion of our drive toward self-realization. It is a betrayal of who we were meant to be, a fall into self-estrangement based on strong feelings of unacceptability. For instance, on another occasion, Horney describes the search for glory this way: "Although destructive in its consequences, it nevertheless stems from man's best desires—to expand beyond his narrow confines. It is, in the last analysis, its colossal egocentricity that distinguishes it from healthy strivings."[53]

While healthy striving stems from an inherent motivation to grow, to progress and to accomplish, this search for glory denies limitations, distorts facts and is driven compulsively. While healthy striving is based on the spontaneity of our choices, the search for glory is motivated by a craving for unlimited power. Whether it is the power of authoritative certainty, perfect righteousness or complete goodness, an absolute must be embodied. Anything less is unsatisfactory. This search makes any type of relaxation impossible. There is always something more to do if we are to insure any sense of legitimacy.

NEUROTIC CLAIMS AND ENTITLEMENT

Sometimes the idealized self raises demands not only on the actual self, but on others as well. Excessive, exalted expectations of others, of course, grow out of an exalted view of ourselves. In other words, we expect a lot out of others because we, in our superior place, deserve it. We are entitled to raise demands and make claims on the basis of this superiority. We have a right to never be disappointed by anyone.

Horney describes this process as the development of neurotic claims. In this maneuver, a wish or need is turned into a demand, and it is considered a deep offense if all of our claims are not met. It's simply unfair. The inflated

---

[52]Ibid., p. 34.
[53]Ibid., p. 176.

commands emerging from a general sense of entitlement are directed toward other people, institutions and life itself.

These neurotic claims look very much like a spoiled child. However, Horney insists that this is not a fair comparison for the child. Calling an adult with this type of entitlement "infantile" overlooks the fact that the infant has not developed the capacity to understand others' needs and limits. Small children know nothing of a mother's need for sleep, for instance. Neurotic adults do not have this cognitive limitation. Yet the compulsivity of their neurotic claims insist that we stop what we are doing and immediately take care of their entitled needs. After all, they have a cosmic right for things to come to them without any effort. Paris offers the following comment about neurotic claims:

> Claims also involve the expectation that we will receive whatever we need to make our solution work. Among the things that self-effacing people expect are love, protection, understanding, sympathy, loyalty, and appreciation of their goodness. Arrogant-vindictive people feel entitled to exploit others with impunity and without guilt. Narcissists require unconditional love and adoration from their fellows, easy superiority, and unvarying good luck. Perfectionists demand "respect for others rather than glowing admiration" and a just reward for their rectitude. Resigned people feel entitled to privacy; no one should expect anything of them and they ought to be "exempt from having to make a living" and assume responsibilities.[54]

The neurotic claims are always self-serving—or I should say, serving of the idealized self.

GENUINE SELF-ESTEEM AND NEUROTIC PRIDE

What, then, are the differences between authentic self-confidence and neurotic pride? Horney says that the two "often feel and look so much alike that an understandable confusion is created in most minds about their differences."[55] How might we distinguish them? Using Horney as a guide, I have outlined their key differences in the table on page 142.

---

[54]Paris, *Karen Horney*, p. 208.
[55]Ibid., p. 87.

Healthy Self-Esteem	Neurotic Pride
Healthy self-esteem is based on a realistic assessment of oneself.	Neurotic pride is based on the creation of an imaginary self with glorified characteristics one "ought" to have.
Healthy self-esteem pursues goals in harmony with one's true being and potential.	Neurotic pride creates a false self that searches relentlessly for glory and triumph.
Healthy self-esteem rests primarily on qualities of character.	Neurotic pride rests primarily on accomplishments, attainments or relationships that have prestige value.
Healthy self-esteem acknowledges and accepts personal faults and liabilities without losing self-respect and self-love.	Neurotic pride claims unbounded virtues but needs constant affirmation, is easily hurt and is self-depreciating.
Healthy self-esteem accepts reality as it is.	Neurotic pride feels entitled to special favor, privilege and immunity.
Healthy self-esteem recognizes and accepts moral limitations and fallibility.	Neurotic pride minimizes actual moral flaws and magnifies the value of mere intellectual assent to high ideals.
Healthy self-esteem recognizes the activities of one's personal "dark side."	Neurotic pride denies, suppresses or ignores these issues, projects them onto others or justifies them as necessary for survival.
Healthy self-esteem may suffer a temporary sense of guilt and regret when one does not live up to his or her ideals.	Neurotic pride wallows in shame, humiliation and self-contempt when one falls short.
Healthy self-esteem is concerned more about reality than image.	Neurotic pride is concerned more about image than reality.
Healthy self-esteem can embrace personal failure without feeling panic or rage.	Neurotic pride cannot endure anything less than perfection without extreme self-recrimination.
Healthy self-esteem accepts vulnerability.	Neurotic pride despises vulnerability and lashes back vindictively when pride is wounded.
Healthy self-esteem accepts responsibility for oneself.	Neurotic pride forgets, justifies, explains away or blames others for personal failure.

It is crucial to remember that neurotic pride is based on attributes that one has arrogated to him- or herself. Put another way, they are qualities only in the imagination. The desire to have a profound self-confidence without any self-development is sometimes obvious in American society. Self-esteem becomes a new form of entitlement. We have a *right* to feel good about ourselves even if we have done nothing to improve and cultivate any of our abilities. We are entitled to a glowing self-concept. Yet trying to feel good about a completely undeveloped self is like trying to feel proud of a home that is falling in. Fantasies of glory do not compensate for a lack of work on the actual self and its genuine potential. Instant self-esteem has about as much depth as the self-help books that market a quick-fix approach.

This seems to be a psychological version of what Bonhoeffer frequently called "cheap grace." The point of self-acceptance is further self-development. As we genuinely acknowledge and accept who we are *now*, we are propelled toward further self-realization, not self-stagnation. Just as faith without works is dead, so self-acceptance without further self-development is meaningless.

HORNEY'S CONTRIBUTION TO THE PRIDE VERSUS SELF-CONTEMPT DEBATE

We have seen how Horney's exploration into basic anxiety, the three movements or "solutions" to that anxiety, the idealized self, the neurotic claims, the sense of entitlement and the rejection of the actual self offer helpful insights into the relationship between pride and self-contempt. Sometimes overlooked, Horney's observations provide a brilliant analysis of the self's struggle with exaltation and disgust.

Horney supports Rogers in her view that basic anxiety and a desire to gain acceptance push us to create the idealized self. This is a rather urgent drive. We arrogate properties to our idealized self because we are convinced that the actual self is not enough. We fear that we cannot make it on the basis of the actual self. It seems too pitiful to be deliberately prideful. Again, this interpretation appears to match the Rogerian conviction that low self-esteem or self-contempt is primary.

Yet particularly in her later writing, Horney argues that out of basic anxiety, unsatisfied with the real self, we create a false self rooted in neurotic pride.

The primary characteristic of neurotic pride is that it refuses to live within the limitations of the actual self. This desire to escape the confines of the actual self and to live out of the fictitious idealized self sounds like Niebuhrian pride. It hates its own limits. As Horney puts it, "Man in reaching out for the Infinite and Absolute also starts destroying himself."[56] This anxiety does not have to be handled this way. For Horney, this path of false pride is the path of all neurotics; for Niebuhr it is the path of everyone. In other words, the more severe neurotic manifests a colorful portrait of the pattern in all of us.

In addition, Horney's three movements, with their idealized solutions, seem to match the patterns identified by Niebuhr. Obviously, the dominant pattern described in *The Nature and Destiny of Man* depicts Horney's movement against others. A preoccupation with power, status, knowledge or moral supremacy clearly matches Horney's "expansive solution." Aggressive self-expression dominates others in an attempt to stamp out the anxiety built into our finitude. Horney offers a graphic description of the power-hungry person:

> He glorifies and cultivates in himself everything that means mastery. Mastery with regard to others entails the need to excel and to be superior in some way. He tends to manipulate or dominate others and to make them dependent upon him. This trend is also reflected in what he expects their attitude toward him to be. Whether he is out for adoration, respect, or recognition, he is concerned with their subordinating themselves to him and looking up to him. He abhors the idea of his being compliant, appeasing, or dependent.[57]

On the other hand, moving toward others in self-surrender matches Niebuhr's discussion of a form of sensuality—namely, the idolizing of another person as the center of our existence. Having lost our centeredness in God, we turn a partner into a deity.

Another Niebuhrian expression of sensuality could be identified with Horney's "moving away" group. The problem here is escape from self through some form of detached activity. Whether it be the use of chemicals,

---

[56]Horney, *Neurosis and Human Growth,* p. 154.
[57]Ibid., p. 214.

compulsive use of the Internet or the self-avoidant watching of television, the hope is to escape the confusions, ambiguities and turmoils of human life by drowning ourselves in some process of disengagement.

Horney would no doubt agree with feminist theologians that Niebuhr has emphasized the "moving against" type of anxiety resolution at the expense of the others, an emphasis that does not adequately address the issues of women. However, she would agree with Niebuhr that even in the movement toward people and away from people, pride is at work. But what kind of pride? It certainly does not look like the bold conceit we often connect with pride. Yet Horney would lead us back to the idealized self that is fueling an unconscious pride system operative even in the most self-effacing behavior. As we have seen, believing that we must be the utmost in selflessness, self-giving and generosity is a form of pride. We must be "above" the human dilemma of having needs or feeling concerned for ourselves. Instead, we are driven by an inflated, idealized self who says we should be *more* patient than others, *more* giving than is humanly possible, *more* self-neglecting than anyone else. What is telling us that we "must" be more than human? It is our own pride system. The very extent to which we condemn ourselves for not achieving all these things is, in part, an indication of an exalted self-expectation. "Expecting too much of ourselves" can involve a subtle form of pride.

This seems harsh to say. It may seem unfair to those suffering from low self-esteem. Yet before we can develop a healthy view of ourselves, we must often dismantle the idealized self and its pride system. The grandiosity of the idealized self must be deflated if we are to care for ourselves in a constructive way.

The point is that the issue of pride and self-contempt are irrevocably bound together. In *Neurosis and Human Growth,* Karen Horney says simply, "pride and self-hate are actually one entity."[58] In other words, we cannot have self-hate if there is not a pride system already intact. To quote Bernard Paris, "Self-hate is the end result of the pride system."[59] The complexities of this pride/self-hate process involve the mark of neurotic pride even in the most self-effacing solution, and the mark of low self-esteem even in the most self-expansive solution. It's not an either-or issue, as the

---

[58]Ibid., p. 110.
[59]Paris, *Karen Horney,* p. 212.

initial polarities of Rogers versus Niebuhr would have us believe.

In describing this dual problem of pride and self-contempt, Horney says, "They result from a dilemma caused by sweeping acclaim on the one hand and active self-disgracing or self-defeating forces on the other."[60] Clinicians treating narcissism have convincingly pointed toward the fragile, vulnerable self beneath the attempts at exaltation. Indeed, insecurity underlies pride. Yet it is also true that beneath much self-belittling, nonassertiveness and self-contempt is a pride system. In other words, beneath the self-derogatory attitude is an idealized self. Maybe this idealized self is fixated on eternal patience, imperturbability or constant self-sacrifice, but the point is that it is fueled by a self-expectation that transcends the limits of being human.

It is here that Horney's work is very helpful in psychologically grasping Niebuhr's point, while at the same time fully appreciating Rogers's work with people full of self-condemnation and self-loathing. I can't stand myself because I am not the self I "should" be. Yet the self I "should" be is constructed out of an unconscious pride system. For Horney, neither pride nor self-contempt stand alone. Lurking in the shadows of one attitude, we can also find the other.

Horney's intricate and comprehensive theory concerning this reciprocal relationship of pride and self-contempt makes it very difficult to accept David Myers's conclusion that people simply think too highly of themselves, period. As we saw in chapter one, Myers believes that the "self-serving bias" encountered during interviews or questionnaires with people is the final word on how they think about themselves. Yet it seems unlikely that this conscious self-report tells the whole story of the individual's self-estimation. Myers apparently sees no significance in unconscious factors or explanatory compensations for feelings of self-contempt that may tug at a person. Quick questionnaires asking for self-evaluation may not get at what is really going on within people. The positive self-evaluations may well be an attempt to defensively mask an underworld of self-doubt. I agree with Myers that low self-esteem is an overused, one-sided diagnosis. Yet I also believe that a pride diagnosis, without an understanding of its relationship to self-contempt, is equally one-sided.

---

[60]Horney, *Neurosis and Human Growth*, p. 140.

One of the tasks of therapy is to help clients get below the compensatory level of self-justification and talk about the more basic explanations they hold about their behavior. This was artistically illustrated in the film *Good Will Hunting*. From a sociological survey of Will Hunting's (played by Matt Damon) self-perception, we would have concluded that he suffered from excessive self-regard. After all, he appeared arrogant, full of himself and exceedingly proud of his intelligence. Yet his therapist, Sean (played by Robin Williams), patiently waited for his compensatory braggadocio to subside so that he could talk about his deeper feelings of inadequacy. Clearly, he used his intelligence to defensively keep his self-contempt at bay.

In summary, we must acknowledge that anxiety precedes both pride and self-contempt. Anxiety, in that sense, is indeed the primary issue. Yet anxiety does not have to be mishandled or misinterpreted. Put theologically, there is nothing intrinsically sinful about our finite existence. While anxiety may whisper the possibility of inadequacy, it is the measuring of the actual self by the unrealistic standards that brings on the judgment of inadequacy. And Niebuhr would quickly add that anxiety only becomes a dysfunctional problem when we fail to trust. It is this fundamental distrust or "unfaith" that requires compensatory, compulsive behavior to convince ourselves that all is well.

Thus, Horney's work suggests that the Augustinian tradition, with its emphasis on pride, needs the feminist corrective and the Rogerian emphasis on the power of self-disgust. Yet her work also suggests that the low self-esteem or undervalued-self emphasis needs the wisdom of the Augustinian emphasis on pride. Horney masterfully points out that the "pride system" within each of us is far more subtle than we might think. Where we see pride or low self-esteem in the foreground, we'll usually find its opposite in the background. The relationship, then, is not either-or. In fact, they share a deeply intertwined connection.

7

ANXIETY, SIN AND
SELF-UNDERSTANDING

The easy way to infinite glory is inevitably also the way to an inner hell of self-contempt and self-torment. By taking this road, the individual is in fact losing his soul—his real self.
KAREN HORNEY

I began this investigation with a simple question: Which is primary in the human condition, pride or self-contempt? Put another way, do we human beings tend to overvalue or undervalue ourselves? As we have seen, traditional Augustinian theology, feminist theology and humanistic psychology differ on this issue. We've examined the work of Niebuhr, witnessed his feminist critics and explored the position of humanistic psychologist Carl Rogers. Further, we've attempted to address a deadlock through the work of Karen Horney.

In this final chapter, I want to work toward an integration of the Augustinian-Niebuhrian emphasis on pride with the feminist and humanistic psychology discussion of self-loss and self-contempt. Again, I believe (a) both perspectives are important for an understanding of the human condition and (b) one perspective, in isolation from the other, will imbalance an effective Christian understanding of sin. As I have suggested, it is not an either-or issue.

As pointed out in the last chapter, I believe Karen Horney has greatly aided our appreciation of the wisdom of both the pride and self-contempt perspectives. I now wish to suggest ways in which these two traditions, as expressed in the theological voices of Niebuhr and his feminist critics, might better understand each other. In attempting this bridge between Augustinian-Niebuhrian pride and the feminist emphasis on self-abnegation, it will be important to focus on (1) the relationship between pride and distrust, (2) the distinction between pride as a theological and psychological issue, (3) the breadth of the terms *pride* and *sensuality* as they are used by Niebuhr, (4) the limitations of a male versus female perspective on sin and (5) the difference between saying that we are equally sinful and that we are equally guilty. I do not want to minimize the differences between the Niebuhrian and feminist perspectives, but believing that both make a valuable contribution, I will attempt to show how they might be combined.

Having attempted to achieve a middle ground between Augustinian pride and feminist self-loss, I will then examine what I consider to be the largest problem for an adequate doctrine of sin in Rogers and humanistic psychology. As helpful as the humanistic psychotherapies often are, they do not have an adequate answer to the problem of ontological anxiety. I will argue, in the tradition of Kierkegaard, Niebuhr and Rollo May, that this problem of ontological anxiety is indeed the breeding ground of sin. Further, we do not simply sin out of need-deficiency or low self-esteem. We can also sin out of strength and exaggerated self-regard.

INTEGRATING THE PRIDE AND
SELF-CONTEMPT PERSPECTIVES

Why not simply say that some people struggle with pride while others wrestle with low self-esteem? Cannot both be true, depending on the people we are describing? Some people are arrogant, period. Some people have low self-esteem, period. People are simply different. This approach loses the rich complexity of the human condition by only focusing on one side of the polarity between pride and self-contempt. As I have attempted to show, the issue is more complicated than that. It is frequently pointed out that beneath the conceited behavior of many individuals is a hounding, self-doubting voice of inadequacy. Yet I have also suggested another possibility that is often dreadfully off-limits in the helping professions: the person with low self-esteem may have a pride system lurking in the background. The "obvious" problem of low self-esteem is more subtle and complex than it might first appear. Many therapists understand that the best way to treat inflated people is to direct them back to the insecurity that underlies self-exaltation. I wish to also suggest that persons with low self-esteem may stay stuck in their self-contempt until they see the inherent pride system tyrannizing them.

In the Genesis account, the first couple was tempted to be "more than they were" rather than "less than they were." Surely unrealistic self-demands, expectations for perfection and severe self-scrutiny are born out of a pride system that expects us to extend ourselves beyond our human limits. This reframing of the low self-esteem problem may be shocking to many of us because we've unconsciously grown proud of being so hard on ourselves. Thus, in the midst of my own self-condemnations, perhaps I should raise the question, "Just who do I think I am?" Perhaps I will discover that my feelings of low self-esteem are attached to an implicit pride system with inflated self-expectations. However, my pride system may be harder to give up than I might think.

It is here that Horney's theory is more comprehensive and nuanced than that of Carl Rogers. For Rogers, as we have seen, the problem always boils down to a lack of self-acceptance. In a sense, Horney would agree with this. After all, it is the actual self, not the idealized self, who desperately needs acceptance. Yet Horney believes that arriving at self-acceptance may necessitate excavating the pride system beneath low self-esteem rather than simply supporting people in their biologically unfolding force-for-growth. Put simply, low self-esteem is more complicated than Rogers allows. Rogers does not discuss the other side of low self-esteem. He describes the self-contempt we feel when we measure ourselves against the introjected values of others, but he does not say much about our own elaborate pride system, which keeps the idealized self going. And it may be the dismantling of this underlying pride system that helps us move toward greater self-acceptance. Yet in order to do this, we must see it as our own *pride* and not simply as low self-esteem caused by other people's rigid expectations. We feel lousy about ourselves because we have an inflated picture of ourselves.

To illustrate the double-sidedness of the pride-insecurity dilemma, consider individuals who refuse to see a counselor even though their behavior creates problems for both themselves and others. On the one hand, we can easily say that they are "afraid" of going for therapy, too insecure to admit any weakness before another. Hence, they must have low self-esteem. Yet the other side of this resistance stems from a belief that they do not need therapy. Others may benefit from this service but there is no need for them to go. They are somehow capable of examining themselves without the aid of another. They are self-sufficient. Their underlying pride system tells them they should be able to fix their own problems. Others may be weaker and need professional services, but not them.

So are they too insecure to ask for help or too proud to think they need any help? Probably both. They vacillate back and forth in an ongoing tension. No one "just" has a self-esteem problem; no one "just" has a pride problem. By understanding the inseparable nature of pride and self-contempt, we are able to move away from the question of which pole represents the primary reality. Where we see one, we'll probably find the other. One pole may clearly dominate. Yet, as we begin to probe the underlying structure of the pride versus self-contempt issue, we may discover that both exist simultaneously.

BACK TO NIEBUHR AND FEMINIST UNDERSTANDINGS OF SIN

Reinhold Niebuhr, as a spokesperson for the Augustinian tradition, offers a very insightful analysis of the human problem of pride. Even his feminist critics do not dispute this. Yet it is equally true that his analysis deals almost exclusively with only one form of pride, the pride of inflated self-assertion. Niebuhr recognizes other forms of pride, but says little about them. Considering the historical period in which Niebuhr wrote, with its rise of fascism and proud dictators, this is most understandable. However, as Plaskow and others have pointed out, Niebuhr claims to be offering a portrait of the overall human condition. Feminists certainly have a point that Niebuhr seems to speak primarily to self-promoting men. Again, while Niebuhr recognizes other forms of pride, he does not develop them.

It is important to remember, however, that Niebuhr does discuss the issue of self-abandonment. He believes that when we refuse to be a self, we then fixate on something that helps us avoid selfhood. That something on which we fixate is a God-replacement. It offers "salvation" from the struggle to be a self.

But Plaskow and other feminists ask whether this God-replacement always involves pride. Isn't self-abandonment a problem in its own right?

Niebuhr's response to this question would probably be that all forms of God-replacement are rooted in pride. Why? Because we unduly focus on the self and its anxieties. Pride, for Niebuhr, means self-preoccupation, not merely self-inflation. Our lives become completely wrapped up in trying to find a security that can only be found in God. We replace God with another "god." This new idolatry is an attempt to feel safe.

PRIDE AND DISTRUST

In one way or another, human pride is always related to distrust in our Source. This distrust is the intervening variable between anxiety and pride. There is an exchange between anxiety and pride—namely, the placement of self at the center of one's being instead of God. As Niebuhr put it, "The sin of inordinate self-love thus points to the prior sin of lack of trust in God."[1] Pride can only take place when we have lost our centeredness in God due to this lack of trust. Niebuhr writes so powerfully about personal, social and economic pride in human history that it is easy to overlook the other side of this pride—the distrust in God that places self at the center. As Langdon Gilkey writes in his excellent study of Niebuhr, "Hence, estrangement from God, 'unbelief,' is presupposed as that which transmutes our finitude into a problem. Then anxiety about our life and its meaning becomes the inevitable temptation to sin."[2]

Thus, the other side of pride is "unfaith" or distrust. In fact, we cannot talk about unfaith without talking also about pride. The minute we cease to place our trust in God, we commit the sin of pride. We may feel insecure when we do this. We may feel frightened. We may even do it with some trembling self-doubts. However, we are replacing God and making our own efforts at control as the center of our life. This invariably leads to an excessive focus on our own security.

---

[1] Reinhold Niebuhr, *The Nature and Destiny of Man,* vol. 1 (New York: Charles Scribner's, 1964), p. 252.
[2] Langdon Gilkey, *On Niebuhr: A Theological Study* (Chicago: University of Chicago Press, 2001), p. 103.

This distrust in God perpetuates our anxiety. We attempt to outmaneuver life and find our own "solution" to the problem of anxiety. This is what makes it prideful: we know better than God! We will seize on some type of security apart from the only security that can console us. This is Niebuhrian pride. The more we distrust, the greater our anxiety. The greater our anxiety, the more tempted we are to sin by acting in frantic ways to establish our own security.

Without a trust in God, our own attempts at self-assertion, individuation or self-actualization are off-balance. We lack balance because we are usually overwhelmed by existential anxiety. This anxiety, again, results from our distrust in our Source. Lacking a spiritual centeredness, our self-expressions emerge in distorted forms. Our attempts at assertiveness, for instance, will be limited by the underlying existential anxiety brought on by our distrust in God. This larger, existential problem of anxiety sabotages our attempts at taking control of our lives. Anxious about the ultimate questions of our lives, we are not prepared for the daily tasks that need our nonanxious, assertive attention. Furthermore, it is the very nature of existential anxiety to keep us self-preoccupied. And the only effective remedy for this existential anxiety is a basic trust in our Creator.

This emphasis on the distrust-pride process might help with feminist objections to Niebuhr. Niebuhr makes a very subtle, highly insightful point about the nature of *all* pride. While he may be appropriately challenged for his overemphasis on "male" expressions of pride, his work also contains an understanding of "female" forms of pride that also emerge out of distrust. The self-abnegation involved in my worshipful, self-sacrificing attitude toward another (my partner, for instance) does not eliminate the reality that it is *my* solution, *my* attempt to ultimately control my security, *my* attempt to order my own life around my insecurities. I can even pridefully negate myself. I can depend on my own attempt to "get rid of" the anxiety of being a human by escaping into another. My "self" may seem so fragile and undeveloped that pride is not the appropriate word for me. Nevertheless, as I rely on my own strategies to handle my existential anxiety (rather than trusting God), it is a subtle, indirect form of pride.

Perhaps a way to incorporate the insight of Niebuhr's sometimes male-dominated view of sin with the feminist rebuttal is to notice the difference between *anxious greed,* which seems so epidemic among power-hungry, egocentric men, and *greedy anxiety,* which is a preoccupation with security. The desire for more and more security can indeed be a kind of greed. In fact, the escape from self by living through another can be an attempt to achieve a kind of security of which we are not capable. When women make partners, children or work their sole focus, are they not trying to find a security that can ultimately be found only in God?

I agree with Plaskow, Hampson, Dunfee and Saiving when they insist that many women do not need more lessons on self-sacrifice. Instead, they may need the admonition of courage to have a self. Yet Niebuhr would probably hold on to the word *pride* to describe these women's situation. The reason is that he never separates distrust and pride. By the mere act of distrust we become unduly focused on ourselves and our own security. We cannot find this ultimate security within finitude. It comes only from a trust in the one who brought our lives into being.

PRIDE AND SENSUALITY: A CONFUSION OF TERMS?

At the risk of glossing over genuine differences, I would also like to suggest that a basic problem between Niebuhr and his critics may have to do with semantics as much as anything else. It seems clear to me that Niebuhr uses the words *pride* and *sensuality* differently than we usually think about them today. Niebuhr writes about pride from a theological angle; we usually think about pride from a psychological one. In other words, behind the word *pride,* as we have seen, Niebuhr is already assuming a distrust and break with God as the source of our security. This is pride with a capital P. Arrogance, having a puffed up quality or attempting to dominate others are all forms of pride with a small *p.* Yet there are many other forms of pride with a small *p.* These include self-avoidance or self-abandonment.[3] The point, for Niebuhr, is that pride is self-preoccupying, whether it manifests itself in grandiosity or low self-esteem.

When we use the word *pride* in most conversation, however, it usually

---

[3]Marty Maddox, friend and colleague, has offered me enormous help in understanding these differing views of "pride" in the writings of Niebuhr and Plaskow. See his "Concupiscence: Our Ultimate Addiction" (S.T.M. thesis, Andover Newton Theological Seminary, 1993).

means one of two things. The first use of *pride* is a favorable one. We are told to have pride in our work. By this, we normally refer to self-respect and responsibility. The second use of the word *pride* is associated with arrogance, conceit or thinking that we are somehow better than others. This is self-exaltation. Yet this second use of *pride* reflects only one dimension of what Niebuhr meant by the word *pride*. Connecting the word *pride* with the experience of a soft-spoken, insecure, self-avoidant person seems peculiar and confusing to us. Yet for Niebuhr, we can have a theological problem with pride at the same time that we have a psychological problem with low self-esteem. If he were alive today, perhaps Niebuhr would be more specific in his uses of the word.

It is important to understand the problem of *egoism* (self-preoccupation) as deeper than the problem of *egotism* (self-inflation). Egoism is a kind of bondage of the will that can take many forms. As feminist theologians have rightly pointed out, Christian theology has traditionally addressed problems of *egotism* rather than *egoism*. Egoism's undue focus on self may be grandiose or self-doubting. Either way, it becomes a prison. With this exaggerated focus on ourselves, it is difficult to address others in their own right because we can't get outside the jail of our needs.

This excessive self-involvement is not necessarily love at all. Here Christian theology could benefit from listening closely to psychotherapists who work with self-obsessed, but not self-loving, individuals. While self-preoccupation may be a grave obstacle to loving others, this is hardly self-love. In fact, excessive self-regard is more likely born out of self-contempt.

If the term *pride* is confusing, even more so is the word *sensuality*. Niebuhr uses the word extremely broadly. On the one hand, *sensuality* is used to describe the hedonistic indulgences to which we may feel entitled. On the other hand, the term is used to describe our idolatrous focus on another, or what has been termed codependency in self-help literature. *Sensuality* is also used to describe our self-avoidant preoccupation with the details of life, a kind of busyness that escapes the frightening issues of an inner life. This avoidance can even take the form of seemingly "selfless" social causes. Again, these causes can be used as a way of detouring the inner courage of "being a self." These experiences are too varied to be covered by one word. The common associations with the word *sensuality* are the pursuit of sensual pleasures or self-indulgence. Thus, the word is not broad enough to cover the other understandings to which Niebuhr applies it.

"MANLY" AND "WOMANLY" SIN

While I deeply appreciate the emphasis on women's experience in feminist theologies and do not want in any way to minimize their insights about female consciousness, I am not sure that sin can be so easily divided between "female" and "male" forms. For instance, some women do indeed exhibit the classic traits of Niebuhrian "male" sin. Theologian Ted Peters describes his conversation with women in his classes:

> In the context of studying the nature of sin and evil, I took opportunities to quiz many of my women students. For one thing, I asked them how sin evidences itself in their lives personally. No one who responded blamed all the evil in the world on the male gender. All admitted their own sinfulness. Women are just as susceptible to pride as men, they told me, but their pride does manifest itself somewhat differently. They viewed women as less given to boasting and bravado but more given to narcissism and manipulation.[4]

Furthermore, men may display what some feminists, following Kierkegaard, have called "women's sin," that is, the failure to become a self. Not every male can be described as a prideful self-asserter. In fact, John Raines suggests that because of the very brilliance in Niebuhr's analysis of pride, his other category, "sensuality," remains painfully undeveloped, even for men.[5] Raines quotes Pitney van Dusen's observation, "Niebuhr writes his theology for the strong; not the weak."[6] For these individuals, a flight from self is an unlikely movement. But with modern affluence, argues Raines, a passive, even slothful lifestyle has become common. Far from being drunk with ambition, many have retreated into a world of quiet resignation. The problem here seems to be inordinate self-forgetfulness rather than inordinate self-love. Consequently, Raines concludes, Niebuhr's "keen insight into the self-love, pride and pretentiousness of man needs to be balanced

[4]Ted Peters, *Sin: Radical Evil in Soul and Society* (Grand Rapids, Mich.: Eerdmans, 1994), p. 115.
[5]John Raines, "Sin as Pride and Sin as Sloth," *Christianity and Crisis* 29 (February 3, 1969): 4-8.
[6]Pitney van Dusen, quoted in Raines, "Sin as Pride and Sin as Sloth," p. 5.

with Marx's sensitivity to the self-loss, passivity, and false consciousness that seduce and vitiate mankind from the opposite direction."[7] Thus, for men also, the temptation of selflessness, of not having the courage to be a self, is a reality. These are ambitionless men who often simply want to be left alone. They perform at their jobs and then retreat into their private world of watching television. Self-reflection is unnecessary. They do not want to be bothered, but simply left to themselves. Niebuhrian pride, for them, is too much work.

Feminists may reply, of course, that this male experience of sloth is not the same as women's experience of self-loss. The power structures in our culture are much more available for men's attempts at self-actualization. Patriarchy obviously supports men's efforts in a manner in which it does not encourage women. The choice to not act on these opportunities in an ambitionless manner is not the same as not having the opportunities in the first place.

The question quickly becomes, however, whether *all* men are the beneficiaries of patriarchy's opportunities. Racial and socioeconomic differences certainly do not offer a level playing field for men either. So, while the socialization process may push women and men in different directions for coping with anxiety, other factors also play a significant role.

EQUALITY OF SIN, INEQUALITY OF GUILT

While Niebuhr believed in the universality of sin, he did not think that everyone is equally "guilty."[8] In other words, powerful, prideful oppressors may indeed be more guilty than the oppressed. This point seems especially relevant in regard to the feminist critique of Niebuhr. The aggressive, power-hungry pride of the traditional male, who runs over people in the name of self-promotion, incurs more guilt than the pride that underlies the self-abnegation of many females. Again, oppressors are always more guilty than the oppressed.

For Niebuhr, then, the equality of sin does not mean the equality of guilt. "It is important to recognize that Biblical religion has emphasized this inequality of guilt just as much as the equality of sin"[9] (Is 2:12; 3:14; 26:5;

---

[7] Ibid.
[8] Niebuhr, *Nature and Destiny of Man*, 1:222.
[9] Ibid.

Amos 4:1; 8:4). The fact that all of humanity is in the same boat does not negate the fact that some do far more damage than others.

Unfortunately, some clergy have unwittingly contributed to the suffering of women by emphasizing the universality of sin at the expense of the inequality of guilt. A battered woman, for instance, may be directed toward her own sin rather than the injustice that is being done to her. She leaves the pastor and tells herself that since she is "not without sin," she shouldn't throw stones at her abusive partner. By turning inward, she has been encouraged to ignore the injustice surrounding her. A sloppy and misused notion that we all sin has silenced her before an unjust situation that needs to be confronted.

ANXIETY AND ITS RELATIONSHIP TO SIN

According to much of Christian theology, anxiety pushes each of us toward the temptation of self-exaltation. Yet anxiety itself is not the enemy. Anxiety does not necessarily carry with it a verdict of condemnation, any more than it carries a message of self-affirmation. Sin never springs automatically from anxiety. The insecurity and frailty of human life is an essential part of our combined biological-spiritual nature.

Yet Christian theology declares that we make ourselves the center of the universe (pride), and as a result, our lives become out of balance. Pride is intricately connected to idolatry because it is always a form of God-replacement. Pride cannot be excused or explained away as a product of environmental factors such as bad parenting. The undue self-focus is not strictly necessary, but it *is* inevitable. Niebuhr believes that while this paradox seems impossible, it does indeed reflect our experience. Invariably we sin, yet we do not *have to*.

For much of humanistic psychology, our anxiety problem is not endogenous, not originating within us. It does not emerge as a part of our finitude. The mishandling of anxiety occurs because of what the environment "does" to us and, hence, is situational. We do not act in destructive ways because of the internal temptations connected with our freedom. The underlying assumption seems to be that in a completely nurturing environment, none of us would choose to act in destructive, unhealthy ways. We need a deep valuing of self because we have fallen into patterns of self-disgust and self-hatred. These may be disguised as aggression toward others or arrogance, but the real issue underneath these phony displays is a lack of self-acceptance.

Thus, for most of humanistic psychology, anxiety only becomes a major problem *after* the emergence of incongruence. We would have done fine if others hadn't laid these conditions on us. In fact, other people *cause* our anxiety. But the humanistic psychologies miss this important point: The anxiety born out of human freedom will invariably tempt us to sin, all on its own, even without any outside help. Granted, the pressures, demands, abuses and "conditions of worth" around us make things worse. They may push us in distorted directions. Yet the backbone of the Christian tradition is that we are responsible. Whether strong or weak, whether feeling full of ourselves or deprived, anxiety will tempt us to distrust God. This anxiety-distrust-sin sequence has always been crucial to a Christian understanding of human distortion.

Thus, I believe Carl Rogers and the undervalued-self thesis ignores, or at least minimizes, the role of ontological anxiety. As I previously mentioned, at this point Rogers does not follow his mentor Kierkegaard closely enough. He does not believe that intrapsychic anxiety, without external conditions, will tempt us to act in destructive ways. This is because of his belief that we have only one natural inclination—namely, to move in a self-actualizing manner. Yet there are temptations built into our finitude that tempt us to become more than we are. This is the inevitable byproduct of a combination of nature and spirit.

It is interesting to note here the differences between Rogers and fellow humanistic-existential psychotherapist Rollo May. On the surface, Rogers and May appear to be quite similar in perspective. Both are typically categorized as leaders of "third force" or humanistic-existential psychology; both are strong believers in human freedom; both have been heavily influenced by phenomenology and existential philosophy (particularly the work of Søren Kierkegaard); and both affirm the dignity of human autonomy. Nevertheless, their difference concerning the place of anxiety in human life is substantial. This difference, in turn, has implications for the whole concept of the one-directional actualizing tendency.

May believes that Rogers minimizes the dilemma of ontological or *essen-*

tial anxiety largely because he does not adequately grasp the destructive potential within human nature.[10] For May, in a way similar to Niebuhr,
anxiety primarily results from our capacity for self-transcendence. As we realize that we are going to die and that our choices "define" us, it evokes tre-
mendous insecurity. This anxiety is basic to our being, not simply a result
of socialization. Our creaturely insecurity can be addressed in many different ways, some of which are most destructive. Kierkegaard, using religious
language, frequently said that anxiety is not sin but that it is the *precondition*
for sin.[11] Put psychologically, anxiety is not itself dysfunction, but it is the
springboard of dysfunctional or destructive behavior. Greed, aggression, hypercompetitiveness, selfishness, rampant consumerism, process and substance addictions and so on are often outgrowths of insecurity. Following
his teachers, Paul Tillich and Reinhold Niebuhr of Union Theological
Seminary, May believes that anxiety is essential to our being and, as such,
offers a constant temptation for destructive action. This temptation arises
from within and is not, as Rogers argues, merely a consequence of social or
environmental pressure. For May, there is no mono-directional actualizing
tendency that will pull us out of the destructive temptations offered to us
by our own existence.

Thus, May has less of a romanticized "blossoming self" and far more of
a rugged, existentially challenged self. May agrees with Niebuhr: anxiety is
part of our very being because we are self-conscious creatures, a mixture of
nature and spirit, with the capacity for self-transcendence. Though he is
often associated with humanistic psychology, May would agree with
Browning's characterization of humanistic psychology and anxiety:

> The humanistic psychologists are aware of the reality of anxiety but
> see it predominantly as socially induced. Anxiety is provoked by the
> threats of punishment or separation that powerful parental figures
> make toward their children early in life. Anxiety is primarily exter-
> nally, sociologically, interpersonally, and situationally created; it does

---

[10]Rollo May, "The Problem of Evil: An Open Letter to Carl Rogers," *Journal of Humanistic Psychology*
22, no. 3 (1982): 11.
[11]Søren Kierkegaard, *The Concept of Anxiety*, trans. Reidar Thomte (Princeton, N.J.: Princeton University Press, 1980).

not come forth from some deeper ontological quality in the very nature of human existence.[12]

May is concerned that Rogers's framework minimizes the "burden of freedom" or the struggle for existential decision making. Why? Largely because of Rogers's emphasis on the biological, instinctual pattern of the actualizing tendency. For May, even if all external threats are turned into nurturing influences, people can still choose destruction out of their essential or ontological anxiety. The reduction of situational anxiety does not mean that a more basic form of anxiety will not emerge.

May believes that each of us experiences anxiety precisely because we do not have a singular actualizing urge (grounded in biology), as Rogers proclaims. Instead, each person has conflicted urges:

> I am stating that I see the human being as an organized bundle of potentialities. These potentialities, driven by the daimonic urge, are the source *both* of our constructive and our destructive impulses. If the daimonic urge is integrated into the personality (which is, to my mind, the purpose of psychotherapy) it results in creativity, that is, it is constructive. If the daimonic is not integrated, it can take over the total personality, as it does in violent rage or collective paranoia in time of war or compulsive sex or oppressive behavior. Destructive activity is then the result.[13]

In contrast, Rogers states an equally direct view:

> I suppose my major difference with Rollo is around the question of the nature of the human individual. He sees the demonic as a basic element in the human makeup, and dwells upon this in his writing. For myself, though I am very well aware of the incredible amount of destructive, cruel, malevolent behavior in today's world—from the threats of war to the senseless violence in the streets—I do not find that this evil is inherent in human nature. In a psychological climate which is nurturant of growth and choice, I have never known an individual to choose the

---

[12]Don Browning, *Religious Thought and the Modern Psychologies* (Philadelphia: Fortress, 1987), p. 85.
[13]Rollo May, "The Problem of Evil: An Open Letter to Carl Rogers," p. 11 (italics in original).

cruel or destructive path. Choice always seems to be in the direction of greater socialization, improved relationships with others.[14]

Rogers goes on to say that his experience has led him to believe that cultural influences are the major factors in evil behavior. The rigors of childbirth, the mixed experience with parents, the negative impact of our educational system and the inequality of wealth and opportunities are all contributing factors. Yet, for Rogers, the presence of these factors does not change the fact that human beings are "*essentially constructive* in their fundamental nature."[15] There is no potential evil element within the human condition.

Yet when Rogers blames culture, our educational system or other social factors for destructive behavior, May quickly asks, "Who makes up all these groups if not individuals?"[16] For May, the mixture of good and evil in culture mirrors the potential good and evil within each individual. The conflict in the social order reflects the internal conflict within each person.

In agreement with May, I believe that each of us must come to terms with ontological, not just interpersonal or situational, anxiety. Even if we have the most ideal nonanxious parents in the world, anxiety will still be built into our human condition. Further, this anxiety is a problem because we each have inherent tendencies toward *both* actualization and destruction. The simple fact that these dual inclinations exist, quite apart from social influence, produces anxiety.

Thus, even if the right therapeutic conditions are originally present, I do not have the Rogerian assurance that I will always move in healthy directions. The actualizing tendency has a potentially destructive twin, and it too, is a powerful force within the psyche. The anxiety built into finitude itself will inevitably awaken this destructive possibility. No one has to "make" me anxious; I will eventually do that all on my own.

SINNING OUT OF STRENGTH AS WELL AS WEAKNESS

Whatever bridges may be built between Christian thought and the human-

---

[14]Carl Rogers, "Notes on Rollo May," *Journal of Humanistic Psychology* 22, no. 3 (1982): 8-9.
[15]Ibid., p. 238.
[16]R. May, "The Problem of Evil," p. 12.

istic psychotherapies, there is an important philosophical difference, which does not easily disappear. Much of contemporary humanistic psychology denies the possibility of personal destructiveness if our basic needs have been met. This is precisely the kind of optimistic view of the human condition about which Christian theology is deeply suspicious. It does not seem to match the facts of human experience. Instead, Christian theology insists that we can sin out of strength as well as weakness.

Let me explain this important point. Humanistic psychologists such as Rogers believe that damaging behavior is an outgrowth of need-deficiency. Something is developmentally lacking within us, which prompts us to act destructively. If our needs are met, we will act cooperatively and harmoniously with others. Yet Christian theology has trouble accepting this optimistic view of human attitudes and behavior. Put simply, we can sin with full bellies as well as empty ones. In the symbolic Genesis account, Adam and Eve did not eat of the forbidden fruit because of need-deficiency. They ate the fruit because they wanted to rise above human finitude and be like God.

Following Augustine, Christian theology says that we sometimes choose destructive behavior for no reason other than our dissatisfaction with human limitations. Sin is not rational. Remember the point of Augustine's famous story about the pear tree.[17] There was absolutely no reason for him to steal the pears. He wasn't hungry and he didn't need them. His desire to steal could not be reduced to a deficiency in his life. Thus, even if all the external conditions of our lives could be perfect, Christian thought insists that we would not escape the temptation to sin. Temptation is not simply an external problem. Rising within our own consciousness is an invitation to move beyond what is humanly possible, distrust our Source and injure many people in our frantic search for justification and security.

Having self-esteem, then, will not end the sin problem. Even when we deeply value ourselves, the anxiety built into finitude will tempt us to find our source of security in some strategy rather than a trust in God.

---

[17]Augustine *Confessions* 2.8-12, trans. Henry Chadwick (New York: Oxford University Press, 1991), pp. 29-31.

CONCLUSION

We have explored two views of the human condition. One view argues that undue self-regard or self-exaltation is the dominant problem of the human condition. Augustine championed this view, which was largely accepted by the Western theological tradition. This "primacy of pride" thesis also finds support from some dimensions of psychology, particularly social psychology. These theorists often emphasize the prevalence of a self-serving bias, a human tendency to exaggerate our own abilities and rate ourselves higher than is warranted. But perhaps the self-exaltation view finds its most powerful contemporary advocate in the writings of Reinhold Niebuhr, particularly in the first volume of his classic statement *The Nature and Destiny of Man*. I have attempted to lay out Niebuhr's perspective as clearly and accurately as I can.

This Augustinian tradition has further asserted that the difficulties of compulsivity, addiction and sensuality are secondary problems created because we have lost our centeredness in God. Once we have pridefully replaced God with our own resolutions to life's anxieties, we are especially vulnerable to unhealthy attachments to finite, limited things. We become addicted to these temporary resolutions because they promise a temporary refuge from the ambiguities and anxieties of being human. We saw in the work of Gerald May a strong restatement of Augustine's view of concupiscence.

Insightful voices within feminist theology have questioned whether or not this Augustinian tradition's emphasis on pride is really the full story, particularly for women. Since Niebuhr is the primary twentieth-century spokesperson for this position, several feminist theologians have criticized him for an overly masculine view of sin as pride, and have suggested that he has not spoken to women's experience.

Niebuhr would probably reply to his feminist critics that the problem of pride is always connected to a distrust in God. Whether or not this distrust involves a puffed-up quality or a shrinking quality, it is still a distrust in our Creator and a reliance on the resources of the self to get rid of the problem of anxiety. For Niebuhr, distrusting God always leads to self-preoccupation. This self-preoccupation may not look like obvious forms of self-aggrandizement (as has been typical of males), yet it always involves a prideful trust in our own resources apart from a trust in God. Thus, pride is primarily a theological problem, which may or may not look like a psychological problem.

Feminists nevertheless contend that the focus of Niebuhr's writings has been too concerned with this self-promoting, arrogant expression of pride. He should not assume it describes women's experience, which has been more of a struggle with *becoming* a self, not worshiping it.

In addition, humanistic psychology, particularly Carl Rogers, who came into direct disagreement with Niebuhr, has been explored. The argument from this perspective states that Niebuhr is not just wrong about women; Niebuhr is wrong about everyone. The Augustinian tradition has led us down a faulty path, and contemporary psychotherapy has shown us that low self-esteem is our most basic problem, not pride.

With much assistance from the work of Karen Horney, I then began to question whether an either-or approach to this issue is comprehensive enough. Instead of asking whether the problem is pride *or* self-contempt, I began to outline the ways in which the two experiences are intricately linked. One may be dominant, but the other does not lie far behind. Thus, there is unexpected low self-esteem in pride and unexpected pride in low self-esteem.

Harshly confronting pride will probably not make it go away any more than lingering with low self-esteem will make it go away. I believe that pastoral theologian Donald Capps is correct when he raises a voice against the moralizing about narcissism in our culture.[18] The prophetic confrontation of our pride also needs an understanding of the other side of pride. This is not to say that our pride does not need to be confronted. Rather, we need a comprehensive understanding of how that pride may be a lot more fragile than it first appears. The calm self-exaltation is based on insecure footing.

I believe that Reinhold Niebuhr knew quite well that beneath the pride to which he often referred cowers a frightened, precarious creature. In fact, this ongoing anxiety is the reason that the declaration of pride becomes even stronger. Pride, as a defensive maneuver, can become so deeply ingrained that only a prophetic challenge or personal crisis may shake it. There are individuals for whom falling on their face appears to be the only way to crack the pride mask. Ego deflation can often be the first step toward grace. And even then, some do not recognize their human vulnerability and need for God.

---

[18]Donald Capps, *The Depleted Self: Sin in a Narcissistic Age* (Minneapolis: Fortress, 1993).

It is also true, however, that therapists working with low self-esteem need to be willing to challenge clients about their underlying pride system and the secondary gains they are getting from the self-contempt. By reframing the low self-esteem issue in such a way that it encourages clients to look at their implicit pride system, they may have a firmer foundation for moving toward self-acceptance. This issue of pride, of course, does not need to be harshly confronted. In some cases, humor can be a helpful strategy. Or the therapist may be quite gentle about it. Nevertheless, sometime during the focus on self-contempt, it is important to begin to deflate the underlying pride system that is causing the self-contempt.

By understanding the inseparable nature of pride and self-contempt, we can move away from the question of which pole represents the primary reality. Where we see one, we find the other. One pole may clearly dominate. Yet, as we begin to probe the underlying structure of the pride/self-contempt issue, we soon discover that its twin is not far away.

From my own experience, I know that most of the time I appear self-inflated, I am really the most insecure. My pretense is deeply related to my insecurity. Moreover, the more painful the self-doubt, the more energy it takes to put up a front of false confidence. At the same time, when I have been particularly down on myself, it is often because I have internal demands that are being manufactured by my pride system. Behind my apparent low self-esteem is a prideful image of self that insists that I must not be like others. Instead, I must be more than human.

I need the grace of God when I am feeling both self-exaltation and self-contempt. Both experiences are very real. Yet neither experience occurs in isolation from the other. If I search around enough, I'll find insecurity beneath my grandiosity and arrogant expectations beneath my self-contempt. It is enormously liberating to recognize my human limitations, allow God's grace to encourage self-acceptance and strive toward the potential for which I am designed.

I hope that this exploration into the pride and self-contempt issue has helped shed a little light on your journey. In reflecting on our own lives, as well as our work with others, I believe it is important to ask how low self-esteem may be lurking beneath pride and how pride may be hiding beneath low self-esteem.

SELECT BIBLIOGRAPHY

Adler, Alfred. *The Science of Living*. New York: Doubleday, 1969.

Augustine, Saint. *The City of God*. Book 4. Translated by Henry Bettenson. London: Penguin, 1984.

———. *Confessions*. Translated by Henry Chadwick. New York: Oxford University Press, 1991.

Barrett-Lennard, Godfrey T. *Carl Rogers' Helping System: Journey and Substance*. London: Sage Publications, 1998.

Barth, Karl. *Church Dogmatics, 3/4, 4/1*. Edinburgh: T & T Clark, 1961, 1956.

Bradshaw, John. *Healing the Shame That Binds You*. Deerfield Beach, Fla.: Health Communications, 1988.

Browning, Don S. *Atonement and Psychotherapy*. Philadelphia: Westminster Press, 1966.

———. *Religious Thought and the Modern Psychologies: A Critical Conversation in the Theology of Culture*. Philadelphia: Fortress, 1987.

Campbell, Donald. "On the Conflict Between Biological and Social Evolution and Between Psychology and Moral Tradition," *American Psychologist* 30 (December 1974): 1103-26.

Capps, Donald. *The Depleted Self: Sin in a Narcissistic Age*. Minneapolis: Fortress, 1993.

Carnes, Patrick. *Out of the Shadows*. Minneapolis: CompCare, 1988.

Christ, Carol P., and Judith Plaskow, eds. *Womanspirit Rising: A Feminist Reader in Religion*. San Francisco: HarperSanFrancisco, 1979.

Cooper, Terry D. "Karl Marx and Group Therapy: An Old Warning About a New Phenomenon." *Counseling and Values* 29, no. 1 (1984): 22-26.

———. "The Psychotherapeutic Evangelism of John Bradshaw." *Pastoral Psychology* 44, no. 2 (1995): 73-82.

———. "Self-Awareness or Self-Absorption: How the Sociology of Knowledge Can Help Counselors." *Counseling and Values* 26, no. 4 (1982): 275-80.

Dodgen, Doreen J., and Mark R. McMinn. "Humanistic Psychology and Christian Thought: A Comparative Analysis." *Journal of Psychology and Theology* 14 (1986): 194-202.

Duffy, Stephen J. *The Dynamics of Grace: Perspectives in Theological Anthropology.* Collegeville, Minn.: Michael Glazier, 1993.

Dunfee, Susan Nelson. "The Sin of Hiding: A Feminist Critique of Reinhold Niebuhr's Account of the Sin of Pride." *Soundings* 65 no. 3 (1982): 316-26.

Evans, Richard I. *Carl Rogers: The Man and His Ideas.* New York: E. P. Dutton, 1975.

Evans, Robert F. *Pelagius: Inquiries and Reappraisals.* New York: Seabury Press, 1968.

Farson, Richard. "Carl Rogers, Quiet Revolutionary." In *Carl Rogers: The Man and His Ideas.* By Richard Evans. New York: E. P. Dutton, 1975.

Finger, Thomas N. *Self, Earth and Society: Alienation and Trinitarian Transformation.* Downers Grove, Ill.: InterVarsity Press, 1997.

Fosdick, Harry Emerson. *As I See Religion.* New York: Harper & Row, 1932.

———. *On Becoming a Real Person.* New York: Harper & Row, 1943.

Freud, Sigmund. *Civilization and Its Discontents.* Translated by James Strachey. New York: W. W. Norton, 1963.

———. *The Ego and the Id.* Translated by James Strachey. New York: Norton, 1962.

Fromm, Erich. *The Art of Loving.* New York: Harper & Row, 1956.

Gilkey, Langdon. *On Niebuhr: A Theological Study.* Chicago: University of Chicago Press, 2001.

———. *Shantung Compound: The Story of Men and Women Under Pressure.* New York: Harper & Row, 1966.

Greenson, Ralph. *The Technique and Practice of Psychoanalysis.* New York: International Universities Press, 1968.

Gross, Martin, L. *The Psychological Society.* New York: Simon & Schuster, 1978.

Hampson, Daphne. "Reinhold Niebuhr on Sin: A Critique." In *Reinhold Niebuhr and the Issues of Our Time.* Edited by R. Harries. Grand Rapids, Mich.: Eerdmans, 1986.

Horney, Karen. *Neurosis and Human Growth.* New York: W. W. Norton, 1950.

———. *Our Inner Conflicts.* New York: W. W. Norton, 1945.

———. *Self-Analysis.* New York: W. W. Norton, 1942.

Horton, Walter. "Reinhold Niebuhr and Carl Rogers: A Discussion by Bernard Loomer, Walter Horton, and Hans Hoffmann." In *Carl Rogers—Dialogues: Conversations with Martin Buber, Paul Tillich, B. F. Skinner, Gregory Bateson, Michael Polanyi, Rollo May, and Others.* Edited by Howard Kirschenbaum and Valerie Land Henderson. Boston: Houghton Mifflin, 1989.

Hugo, John. *St. Augustine on Nature, Sex, and Marriage*. Chicago: Scepter Press, 1969.

Jones, Serene. *Feminist Theory and Christian Theology: Cartographies of Grace*. Minneapolis: Fortress, 2000.

Kaminer, Wendy. *I'm Dysfunctional, You're Dysfunctional: The Recovery Movement and Other Self-Help Fashions*. New York: Vintage, 1993.

Kaufman, Gershen. *Shame: The Power of Caring*. Rochester, Vt.: Schenkman, 1980.

Kavanaugh, John F. *Following Christ in a Consumer Society*. Maryknoll, N.Y.: Orbis, 1981.

Kierkegaard, Søren. *The Concept of Anxiety*. Translated by Reidar Thomte. Princeton, N.J.: Princeton University Press, 1980.

Kirschenbaum, Howard. *On Becoming Carl Rogers*. New York: Delta Books, 1979.

Kirschenbaum, Howard, and Valerie Land Henderson, eds. *Carl Rogers—Dialogues: Conversations with Martin Buber, Paul Tillich, B. F. Skinner, Gregory Bateson, Michael Polanyi, Rollo May, and Others*. Boston: Houghton Mifflin, 1989.

Kohlberg, Lawrence. "Development as the Aim of Education." *Harvard Educational Review* 42, no. 4 (1972): 449-95.

Kurtz, Ernest. *Not-God: A History of Alcoholics Anonymous*. Center City, Minn.: Hazelden Foundation, 1979.

Lasch, Christopher. *The Culture of Narcissism*. New York: W. W. Norton, 1979.

———. "Sacrificing Freud." *New York Times Magazine*. February 22, 1976.

Lears, T. J. Jackson. *No Place for Grace: Antimodernism and the Transformation of American Culture, 1880-1920*. Chicago: University of Chicago Press, 1994.

Maddox, Marty Miller. "Concupiscence: Our Ultimate Addiction." S.T.M. thesis, Andover-Newton Theological Seminary, 1993.

May, Gerald. *Addiction and Grace*. San Francisco: Harper & Row, 1988.

May, Rollo. "The Problem of Evil: An Open Letter to Carl Rogers." *Journal of Humanistic Psychology* 22, no. 3 (1982): 10-21.

McCormick, Patrick. *Sin as Addiction*. Mahwah, N.J.: Paulist, 1989.

Mercandante, Linda. *Victims and Sinners*. Louisville, Ky.: Westminster John Knox, 1996.

Miles, Margaret. *Desire and Delight: A New Reading of Augustine's Confessions*. New York: Crossroad, 1992.

Myers, David, G. *The Inflated Self*. New York: Seabury, 1980.

———. *Social Psychology*. 5th ed. New York: McGraw-Hill, 1996.

Myers, David, and Malcolm Jeeves. *Psychology Through the Eyes of Faith*. San Francisco: Harper & Row, 1987.

Niebuhr, Reinhold. "Human Creativity and Self-Concern in Freud's Thought." In *Freud and the Twentieth Century*. Edited by Benjamin Nelson. New York: Meridian, 1957.

———. *An Interpretation of Christian Ethics*. New York: Harper & Brothers, 1935.

———. *The Nature and Destiny of Man*. 2 vols. New York: Charles Scribner's Sons, 1964.

———. *The Self and the Dramas of History*. New York: Charles Scribner's Sons, 1955.

Oakland, James A. "Self-Actualization and Sanctification." *Journal of Psychology and Theology* 2 (1974): 202-9.

Oden, Thomas C. *Care of Souls in the Classic Tradition*. Philadelphia: Fortress, 1984.

———. *Kerygma and Counseling*. Philadelphia: Westminster Press, 1966.

———. *The Structure of Awareness*. Nashville: Abingdon, 1969.

Paris, Bernard J. *Karen Horney: A Psychoanalyst's Search for Self-Understanding*. New Haven, Conn.: Yale University Press, 1994.

Peale, Norman Vincent. *The Art of Living*. New York: Abingdon-Cokesbury, 1937.

Pelagius. "Letter to Demetrius." In *Theological Anthropology*. Edited and translated by J. Patout Burns. Philadelphia: Fortress, 1981.

Peters, Ted. *Playing God? Genetic Determinism and Human Freedom*. New York: Routledge, 1997.

———. *Sin: Radical Evil in Soul and Society*. Grand Rapids, Mich.: Eerdmans, 1994.

Plaskow, Judith. *Sex, Sin, and Grace: Women's Experience and the Theologies of Reinhold Niebuhr and Paul Tillich*. Lanham, Md.: University Press of America, 1980.

Raines, John. "Sin as Pride and Sin as Sloth." *Christianity and Crisis* 29 (February 3, 1969): 4-7.

Ricoeur, Paul. *The Symbolism of Evil*. Translated by Emerson Buchanon. Boston: Beacon Press, 1967.

Roberts, Robert C. "Carl Rogers and the Christian Virtues." *Journal of Psychology and Theology* 13 (1985): 263-73.

Rogers, Carl R. "Autobiography." In *A History of Psychology in Autobiography*. Edited by E. G. Boring and G. Lindzey. New York: Appleton-Century-Crofts, 1967.

———. *Client-Centered Therapy*. Boston: Houghton Mifflin, 1951.

———. "Concluding Comment." In *Carl Rogers—Dialogues: Conversations with Martin Buber, Paul Tillich, B. F. Skinner, Gregory Bateson, Michael Polanyi, Rollo May, and Others*. Edited by Howard Kirschenbaum and Valerie Land Henderson. Boston: Houghton Mifflin, 1989.

———. *On Becoming a Person*. Boston: Houghton Mifflin, 1962.

———. "Reinhold Niebuhr's *The Self and the Dramas of History*." *The Chicago Theo-

logical Seminary Register no. 1 (1956); reprinted in *Carl Rogers—Dialogues: Conversations with Martin Buber, Paul Tillich, B. F. Skinner, Gregory Bateson, Michael Polanyi, Rollo May, and Others.* Edited by Howard Kirschenbaum and Valerie Land Henderson. Boston: Houghton Mifflin, 1989.

———. "Reply to Rollo May's Letter to Carl Rogers." *Humanistic Psychology* 22, no. 4 (1982): 85-89.

———. "A Theory of Therapy, Personality, and Interpersonal Relationships as Developed in the Client-Centered Framework." In *Psychology: A Study of a Science.* Vol. 3, *Formulations of the Person and the Social Context,* pp. 184-256. Edited by S. Koch. New York: McGraw-Hill, 1959.

Rogers, Carl R., and Barry Stevens. *Person to Person: The Problem of Being Human.* New York: Pocket Books, 1971.

Rubin, Theodore Isaac. *Compassion and Self-Hate.* New York: David McKay, 1975.

Ruether, Rosemary Radford. *Sexism and God-Talk.* Boston: Beacon, 1983.

Saiving, Valerie. "The Human Situation: A Feminine View." In *Womanspirit Rising: A Feminist Reader in Religion.* Edited by Carol P. Christ and Judith Plaskow. San Francisco: HarperSanFrancisco, 1979.

Schur, Edwin. *The Awareness Trap: Self-Absorption Instead of Social Change.* New York: McGraw-Hill, 1976.

Sykes, Charles. *A Nation of Victims: The Decline of American Culture.* New York: St. Martin's Press, 1992.

Tillich, Paul. *The Courage to Be.* New Haven, Conn.: Yale University Press, 1952.

Van Belle, Harry A. *Basic Intent and Therapeutic Approach of Carl R. Rogers.* Toronto: Wedge Publishing, 1980.

Van Leeuwen, Mary Stewart. *Gender and Grace.* Downers Grove, Ill.: InterVarsity Press, 1990.

Vanderpool, Harold Y. "Reinhold Niebuhr: Religion Fosters Social Criticism and Promotes Social Justice." In *Critical Issues in Modern Religion.* By Roger A. Johnson, Ernest Wallwork, Clifford Green, H. Paul Santmire and Harold Y. Vanderpool. Englewood Cliffs, N.J.: Prentice-Hall, 1973.

Vitz, Paul C. *Psychology As Religion: The Cult of Self-Worship.* 2nd ed. Grand Rapids, Mich.: Eerdmans, 1994.

Author Index

Subject Index